Countertrade, Barter, And Offsets

New Strategies for Profit in International Trade

Countertrade, Barter, And Offsets

New Strategies for Profit in International Trade

Pompiliu Verzariu

McGraw-Hill Book Company

New York St. Louis San Francisco Auckland Bogotá
Hamburg Johannesburg London Madrid Mexico
Montreal New Delhi Panama Paris São Paulo
Singapore Sydney Tokyo Toronto

Library of Congress Cataloging in Publication Data

Verzariu, Pompiliu.
Countertrade, barter, and offsets.

Includes index.
1. Countertrade. 2. Barter. I. Title.
HF1412.V47 1985 658.8'48 84-14385
ISBN 0-07-067331-4

1234567890 DOC/DOC 8987654

ISBN 0-07-067331-4

The editors for this book were William A. Sabin and Anne McCoy, the designer was Dennis Sharkey, and the production supervisor was Reiko F. Okamura. It was set in Baskerville by Centennial Graphics, Inc. Printed and bound by R. R. Donnelley & Sons Company.

The views expressed in this text are those of the author and do not necessarily represent those of the U.S. Department of Commerce.

The pronouns "he" and "his," as well as terms such as "businessman," have been used in this book to avoid awkward grammatical constructions and do not reflect bias on the part of author or publisher.

To Tonina, Cristina,
and Giulia, my personal guiding constellation

About the Author

Prior to forming his own trade consulting firm, Pompiliu Verzariu was a business counselor in the International Trade Administration of the U.S. Department of Commerce. For nearly a decade he has advised U.S. firms on structuring specific countertrade transactions and on organizing in-house countertrade units.

Since 1981, he has held annual lectures on countertrade and joint ventures at the National Center for Science and Management of the Dalian Institute of Technology in the People's Republic of China.

Dr. Verzariu is the author of the widely read and translated primer, *Countertrade Practices in East Europe, the Soviet Union, and China* (U.S. Department of Commerce).

Contents

Preface

The past decade has witnessed a succession of political, economic, and monetary instabilities in many areas of the world. As a result of the change in world economic conditions which the energy crisis initiated in the mid-1970s, the economic growth of many developing countries has been stymied.

The uneven distribution and increasingly impaired flow of financial, technical, and natural resources between the world's nations have driven an expanding number of developing countries to impose conditions on western exporters, linking imports of western goods with exports of their domestic products. This compensatory initiative is supposed to open new export markets for developing nations (thereby alleviating trade and payment imbalances), support the industrialization efforts of these countries, and remedy their lack of foreign exchange. Because of economic pressures, compensatory requirements are occasionally imposed by industrialized countries with deteriorating economies in their trade with other developed nations.

The specter of compensatory demands confronts many exporting firms with prospects they are not equipped to handle, especially small firms or those specializing in a single product. Concern about the impact of compensatory practices on a company's exports is now graduating from the export manager's tier to the company's corporate boardroom. Indeed, increasing compensatory pressures in the marketplace (as well as intensified competition for export market shares which has resulted from the slowdown in world trade) require that U.S. exporters be at least conversant with basic notions about the practice. They will need to know how to cope with it if they are to compete successfully in world markets and attempt to turn imposition into opportunity.

This book is intended to acquaint private-sector company executives and public officials with basic information about the practice and to make them more knowledgeable about compensatory obligations that they may face. Because each compensatory arrangement is responsive to the evolving needs of the parties involved, its structure varies as a function of country, product, and time. Relying on creative financing and marketing, the structure of such an arrangement most often defies a precise model.

Facts and figures related to the global expansion of compensatory practices are at present changing as a function of the trading parties' learning processes, their perceptions of need, and the proposed uses for such arrangements (e.g., as related to marketing or financing considerations). To compensate for the variable circumstances and applications of compensatory practices in international markets, the reader may best be served by becoming versed in general criteria of preventive or proactive marketing strategies and in the principles of risk assessment related to compensatory transactions. Thus, the following chapters on compensatory trade emphasize reasons and reasoning and aim at the development of planning steps, support services, and an awareness of risks peculiar to compensatory arrangements in general. The reader can then design applications to suit his own specific needs in marketplaces worldwide.

Countertrade, Barter, And Offsets

New Strategies for Profit in International Trade

chapter 1

Compensatory Trade as an International Issue

The post–World War II years saw increased economic interdependence fostered by expanded trade relations among nations with differing political convictions and diverse economic systems. Today, when shrinking export markets, industrial overcapacity, and contraction of international credit are straining the world's trade system, nations are groping to find innovative means to sustain previously achieved trade levels and to redress deteriorating economic conditions.

The inadequacy of financial transfers to compensate for diminishing market-transfer privileges has driven many developing countries and an increasing number of developed countries to impose conditions that link imports of foreign goods with exports of domestic products or conditions that are tied to commitments to maximize the domestic content of the transactions. These compensatory practices foster contractual quid pro quo arrangements designed to:

Alleviate or overcome shortages of foreign exchange

Support the continuation of industrialization programs

Promote exports of counterdelivered goods which may be in low demand in targeted foreign markets

Sustain the goods' export prices in the face of declining demand

The Nature of Current Compensatory Arrangements

Compensatory arrangements (CAs), mostly involving exchanges of products, have found application periodically during times of worldwide economic sluggishness. But while previous bilateral trade tie-ins after the two world wars occurred in environments dedicated to reconstruction, today's arrangements follow more than two decades of sustained economic growth which, aided by expansion of international trade ties and liberal credit, has fostered global economic interdependence and has heightened social aspirations and economic demands by third world countries.

Thus most CAs of today do not lend themselves to the bilateral models tested in the past, which involved primarily exchanges of goods under government-mandated or -abetted agreements. Instead, current CAs have the option of making full use of the international network of commercial and financial linkages established in the last three decades, in order to multilateralize through the inclusion of additional parties located in diverse countries (e.g., a firm's overseas subsidiaries, multinational brokers) what essentially started as a bilateral commitment. Today's CAs, involving on occasion the transfer of services, may require creative marketing and financing approaches that conform to the particular nature of the products traded and to the evolving needs of the contracting parties. Examples are:

Settlements of compensatory obligations by taking advantage of preferential trade arrangements (e.g., by procuring, in part or whole, the exports or by routing related counterdeliveries through subsidiaries of western firms operating in developing countries, thereby benefiting from settlements in soft currencies and from tariff rebates)

Risk-sharing initiatives (e.g., investment by an exporter in the importer's production capacity with the intent to upgrade the quality of the counterdeliveries)

Allocation of the exporter's resources to worldwide brokerage activities that will benefit the importer (e.g., assistance in creating new export opportunities resulting in revenues for the latter)

Not every compensatory transaction involves complex arrangements. Indeed, many CAs are still implemented on a bilateral basis. At the same time, many developing countries considering the adoption of compensatory practices are doing so with circumspection, as they educate themselves in the use of this new tool which is expected to provide them with economic benefits in a world of declining opportunities.

We recognize three stages in the educational evolution of companies and government agencies engaging in CAs. In the first stage, the trading parties attempt to conclude transactions with little or no outside guidance or assistance. Inexperience and overestimation of ability to perform render many of the contracted arrangements uneconomical. In this stage, the importing government's attitude is to shift all risk associated with the marketing of counterdelivered goods to the western exporter. Many east-west trade CAs negotiated in the late 1960s fell within this category. In the second stage, additional parties (e.g., traders, brokers) are looked upon for assistance from the early stages of negotiations. For the importing countries, government involvement entails administrative directives or resolutions intended to create guidelines for compensatory transactions in which their nationals engage. Most current CAs fall in this category. Finally, in the third stage, compensatory strategies become part of the planning process of both importers and exporters. The CA options explored by the trading parties may include utilization of the importer's production resources in the transaction, investment, and financing schemes, as well as sourcing and routing goods, components, and equipment so as to reduce the importer's net outlays of foreign exchange. For the importing countries, government involvement entails active assistance to the CA by facilitating, for example, the sourcing of counterdeliveries from diverse industrial sectors of the country. This category corresponds to CAs usually undertaken in the trade between two developed countries involving, for example, military or civil aircraft offset arrangements (see Chapter 4). It is the type of CA that third world countries will strive to imitate in the future.

Types of Compensatory Trade Agreements

In the broadest sense, "compensatory arrangements" refer to a whole range of business arrangements (e.g., coproduction, subcontracting, technology transfer, investment, and export generation) whereby an exporter commits himself contractually to cause or actually generate desired benefits such as revenues for the importer. Under CAs, acceptance on the part of the exporter of such arrangements is imposed by the importer as a condition to import. Thus, a main goal of CAs is to reduce or eliminate, over a stipulated period of time, the net outflow of foreign exchange for importers.

CAs may be dictated by government-sponsored requirements for minimum domestic content for specified foreign imports, as in Australia, or as a condition on foreign investment prescribing export quotas for the resulting production, as in India. CAs may also be implemented under government-to-government bilateral agreements. These agreements may either facilitate the transferal of reciprocal market access privileges between two nations—beyond tariff treatment prerogatives—or may impose conditions intended to redress trade imbalances. Some agreements, in the form of bilateral clearing agreements (e.g., between Brazil and Poland), trade protocols (e.g., Japan and the People's Republic of China), or trade investment treaties (e.g., the Caribbean Basin Initiative promoted by the U.S. government), may stipulate or facilitate trade and investment between two nations under preferential terms, often to the potential detriment of another nation's exports. Other agreements, specifying conditions for reciprocity in the commerce of two nations, may aim at balancing the trade levels of the two countries.

In a narrower sense, CAs involve the linked trade obligations of two commercial enterprises in two countries involving exchanges of products, technology, and services, as stipulated in their import and export contracts. Such offsetting obligations, usually undertaken under separately financed and parallel contracts, may also be encouraged by government policies, as in Norway tying offshore oil concessions to foreign contributions to the development of the Norwegian industry. They could be on a *best-effort* basis, as in some western European countries; involve only government procurement contracts, as in Indonesia; be required for specific industrial sectors, as in Austria; or be required for all foreign trade transactions, as in Romania. These types of CAs, commonly referred to as *countertrade transactions*, will be discussed under their various forms in Chapter 3.

The public sector agreements are intended to integrate economies of particular countries, recognize special political relations existing between two nations, or fulfill national demand for raw material resources. Generally, compensatory agreements are designed to minimize trade and payment imbalances. Such agreements foster bilateralism and tend to introduce rigidities and distortions in the world's economy. Once introduced, these are hard to eradicate, given the inertia inherent in government actions and the domino-like interdependence of nations. In the long run, such agreements are likely to result in shifts in industrial-production capacity and in sourcing from developed to developing countries, and are likely to perpetuate shortcomings in the marketing skills of the latter countries.

Causes and Longevity of Compensatory Trade

Whether the present downturn in the growth of the world's economies is related to the long-term economic cycles predicted by the Russian economist Nikolai Kondratieff, or whether it can be traced to identifiable socioeconomic causes, the onset of the global economic slowdown coincided with the occurrence of the worldwide energy crisis of the mid-1970s. The crisis signaled an end to the era of cheap energy, which had contributed so much to international industrial growth. It further accentuated already existing uneven flows of financial and technological resources among the world's nations and sired a chain of interrelated events whose consequences are lasting and conducive to bilateral arrangements.

During the late 1970s, oil-importing nations faced with mounting payment deficits found it expedient to finance their deficits through debt rather than through adoption of belt-tightening measures. In doing so, developing countries in particular were encouraged by the willingness of private banks to finance borrowing against future earnings forecast on past performances and were encouraged by western governments' policies providing for liberal credits, subsidies, and guarantees designed to boost exports in the face of shrinking world markets. Political pressures to continue social and industrial modernization programs, conceived during earlier and more prosperous years, also contributed to national debt accumulations, leading to today's situation in which interest on foreign debt constitutes the single biggest drag on the finances of an increasing number of developing nations.

The debt-repayment crunch is forcing nations such as Brazil, Mexico, Argentina, Poland, and Romania to allocate an inordinate portion of their foreign exchange earnings to debt payments rather than imports. Pressures for debt reschedulings are also mounting in other developing countries, as about one-third of total external debt and about half of the commercial bank debt fell due in 1982. It is estimated that the servicing of debt by the world's debtor countries would require an annual export surplus of between $80 and $100 billion. But it is unrealistic to expect the world markets to absorb such a surplus, given current economic conditions. Brazil's near-default in May 1983, as well as the inability of Latin American and other third world debtors to meet their financial targets, leaves little choice to major creditor banks but to scramble reluctantly to arrange additional loan packages for their financially strapped clients at a time when smaller banks are cutting down their credit participation to third world nations. As a result, the specter of default and the problem of repeated debt reschedulings are now straining the world's financing resources to cope with anticipated and unexpected crises.

Today the lending to developing countries by private banks, which carry the bulk of the approximately $800 billion debt these nations now owe (compared with the $100 billion owed in 1973), is slowing sharply. The slowdown is further jeopardizing the developing nations' ability to service interest payments and to sustain economic growth, while it puts added pressure on western governments and international financial institutions such as the International Monetary Fund to expand their lending programs to the third world. The increasingly difficult task of securing the needed bridge-loan financing to service debt, coupled with apprehensions that their countries' futures have been mortgaged to pay foreign bankers, could also tempt some major debtor countries to impose moratoriums on repayments or to impose unilateral debt-rescheduling terms, as Argentina did in 1982.

The credit squeeze is forcing developing nations to revise their previous plans for economic growth which relied on building industrial bases to process raw materials at home. Past policies of import substitution based on capital-intensive heavy industrialization are being shelved in favor of smaller-scale public works projects which are low in foreign exchange cost and are labor-intensive. Economic retrenchment is resulting in imports being slashed, industrial production being crippled, and standards of living being reduced. These factors, as well as mounting unemployment in developing countries with large populations, are raising fears that political instabilities could accompany economic ones if the nations have to endure more than a few years of recession and stagnation.

As a result, many foreign-exchange-poor developing countries are pressing for CAs as a way to carve export markets for their manufactures against protectionistic pressures in sluggish western markets, as a hedge against volatile prices for their commodity exports, and as suasion for investment of foreign resources in local industries. The long-term nature of the economic problems besetting developing countries points to uneven recovery among these nations, tied to their ability to move up on the high-technology ladder of manufacturing and to attract foreign investment. CAs may well provide one of the means for fulfilling the latter goals and be looked upon by these nations as a desirable tool of trade for as long as their credit and exports will be constrained. Given the feeble recovery pace projected for the world's economies, well below the growth experienced in the aftermath of previous recessions, and because of the high debt-service burden carried by the third world, the prospects for global credit relaxation and strong trade expansion for developing nations' exports appear dim in the near term.

The developed nations, upon whose economic growth is predicated any hope for the recovery of the developing countries, are themselves staggering under the triple weight of budget deficits, high real interest rates, and gradual, uneven recovery from recession. Economic recovery in the industrialized countries has already begun, but it is encumbered by excess industrial capacity, which has suffered from competing new capacity established in third world countries; by mounting unemployment, which is projected to approach 9 to 10 percent of the labor force, or about 32 to 35 million people in 1984; and by dismal prospects for exports to the developing countries which are cutting down on their purchases of western goods and services. As trade frictions, sectoral trade restrictions, and protectionistic pressures (the latter hiding under the euphemisms "orderly marketing," "fair trade," and "voluntary restraints") have intensified worldwide, the developed countries are increasingly treating international commerce as an extension of national economic policies and are preferring to deal with problems of trade competition through bilateral accommodations. For example, French and German banks demand that any new loans to Brazil be tied to their countries' exports to Brazil, and countertrade is increasingly promoted by western exporters as a means to circumvent payment restrictions on foreign exchange imposed by developing countries.

Contributing to the erratic international trade flows have been the volatile currency-exchange rates of the industrialized countries, which have been spurred by variations in interest rates prevailing in different markets, shifts in investment patterns, financial speculations, and the countries' different economic policies. Persisting high interest rates in the United States have been drawing in foreign capital, thus contributing at least partially to the strength of the dollar. This in turn has affected the U.S. companies' ability to export and has added to the burden of the developing countries' debt payments, since about 90 to 95 percent of their debt is dollar-denominated. The Organization for Economic Cooperation and Development (OECD) had estimated that each 1 percent rise in interest rates above the 6-month London Interbank Offered Rate—to which most loans to third world countries are tied—costs these nations a staggering $2.5 billion.

Global economic rebound appears to be slow and uneven. The industrial nations' average real growth rate of 3 percent plus, well below the 5 to 6 percent average growth rates attained during recovery phases of previous post–World War II recessions, does not as yet appear to have the momentum to ensure the rebound needed to pull the rest of the world out of economic stagnation and onto the path of renewed economic growth. Whether the current recovery will be durable hinges on the capacity of the industrialized countries to sustain a coordinated pace of growth devoid of protectionism—an arduous task in view of high unemployment and budget deficits. It also depends on the ability of developing countries to put their houses in order in the face of growing domestic social pressures and not to succumb to political instabilities. The uncertainties and tenuous balance of factors required for stable recovery of the interwoven economies of the world nations make it doubtful that the current crisis will be short-lived or that some nations will be able to resist seeking short-term redress cures to payments or trade imbalances through the invocation of reciprocal trade privileges and bilateral arrangements.

Stated differently, the worldwide factors likely to fuel compensatory practices during this decade are: countries lacking foreign exchange; government policies vying to support exports in a competitive trade environment; idle contractors and production capacity; a widening technology gap between the developed and developing nations; and the inadequacy of financial transfers to make up through credits for lagging market transfer privileges.

Trends in Compensatory Trade

During this decade, efforts by western governments to infuse new life into their economies will be conditioned by the following realities:

The economic interdependency of the world's nations, which has evolved as a result of international trade growth in previous decades

The continued commitment by developing nations to their own growth, and the likelihood of political instability in the third world resulting from rising debt

The self-imposed limitations of the international monetary system in coping with the recycling of financial surpluses to needy developing countries

The first reality suggests that economic initiatives in domestic markets, such as financial discipline, may not suffice to restore strength to a country's economy unless such initiatives also take into account the country's foreign trade balance through promotion of exports, even when it entails linked import obligations.

The second reality stresses the necessity to take into consideration the third world's needs and aspirations for continued economic growth through trade. Failure to do so would limit the options of the industrialized nations to partake in the growth potential of the developing markets. It could also result in political instabilities which may open the door to authoritarian, antiwestern regimes in these countries, with incalculable losses of markets and security for the west.

The third reality acknowledges that the need for financial credit has not abated. Yet it also recognizes that the current debt load accumulated by the developing countries poses a formidable challenge to the world's financial institutions and precludes purely financial remedies in restoring strength to international trade.

In the context of these realities, it is clear that programs by western governments that would transfer market-access privileges to developing nations, beyond existing preferential tariff treatments, would be welcomed initiatives to supplement financial transfers to these countries. Indeed, the trend for the 1980s is for more bilateralism under the auspices of government-negotiated trade agreements, as western governments strive to secure advantages in foreign markets for their own exporters against competition from those of other nations.

In taking up the challenge and vying for a presence in the rapidly changing international trade environment of the 1980s, exporters will be increasingly influenced by perceptions of risk. For decisions, they will be forced to rely on flows of market intelligence kept current and provided by private and public sources and will be forced to resort to varied export-assistance expertise residing outside their own companies. Indeed, mustering the necessary resources to exploit opportunities in foreign markets in coming years may result in prohibitive marginal costs for many an exporter. The result may well be a filtering in of the number and types of western companies that can afford to be active in, and match the import priority needs of, developing nations and in selective involvement by these firms in only a handful of the more prosperous and stable markets in the third world.

As CAs proliferate, the success of that fraction which proves to be viable will require creative financing and marketing approaches. For major transactions, it may involve piecing together sources of financing, supplies, and services in different developing and developed countries, and balancing reciprocal trade and cash flows among several international parties in a fashion that would minimize for the importer net outflows of hard currency while maximizing the use of his resources. Thus, the use of CAs may become an accepted option in the planning process for exporters staking out long-term market positions abroad.

Keeping pace with the growth of CA-related assistance by public and private sources providing advisory, market-intelligence, and information-clearing services to exporters will likely call for arrangements allowing:

Transfer of CA-related credits and debits among collaborating exporting firms and those importing goods from developing countries

Services provided by financial institutions or trade brokers facilitating syndication of large CA obligations among several parties, or consolidating several small CAs into larger ones

Creation at some future date of financial instruments tied to specific CA transactions in selected countries, i.e., collateral-backed promissory notes for future counterdeliveries as payment for imports

As for the developing countries, their industrial capacity has been and will be dedicated to exports, not CAs. These countries' interests lie in the acquisition of long-term rather than spot-market outlets for their goods. Thus, the type of CAs encouraged and facilitated by third world governments will be those tied to extended counterdelivery arrangements or to those involving long-term cooperation or investment agreements. The enforcing of these practices—whether legislated or mandated by administrative directives, applying to specific industrial sectors or spanning all sectors—will vary according to the unique character of the needs of individual developing countries. For example, CAs may become a requirement in those industrial sectors which rely on imports of semifinished goods and components from industrialized countries and which lack export markets in the west for their outputs. They may provide the needed alternative for the undertaking of industrial projects for which foreign exchange cannot be made available. They may be a requirement for projects in the public health sector (e.g., hospital construction and equipping) and in the education and science sectors (e.g., laboratory and classroom equipment, computers) which rank high in social importance of developing nations but low in the allocation of hard-currency funds.

As CAs proliferate, they are increasingly becoming an accepted option in the planning process of both western exporters and developing countries. Indeed, western exporters are now actively promoting CAs as a means to circumvent payment restrictions on foreign exchange by developing countries and as a competitive edge against other exporters. At the same time, an increasing number of developing-country governments (e.g., Malaysia, Brazil, Mexico, South Korea) are in the process of studying ways of using CAs to redress deteriorating trade imbalances. Given the inertia implicit to government actions, the limited prospects for economic recovery for many developing countries, and the accommodating attitudes of western exporters competing for shrinking markets, it is likely that CAs will affect international trade flows for many years to come.

The outlook for the 1980s would also indicate that:

Military or civil aviation CAs (offset programs) will continue to be a major portion of CA trade flows because of their high dollar value. Obligations assumed under such programs tie down significant production and market shares worldwide for many years.

CAs involving counterpurchases of agricultural commodities probably will not show significant growth. The established trade and consumption patterns of commodities are adequately fulfilled under existing arrangements, the prices of commodities are volatile and the marketing of a major portion of these commodities is entrenched in the hands of a few brokers. Indeed, inordinate competition or infusion—as a result of counterpurchase arrangements—of significant surplus volumes in the existing balanced commodity trade flows could depress the commodities prices, as a nation's exports resulting from counterpurchases may end competing with its regular exports.

The largest potential growth lies with CAs related to extractive and capital projects and in the light-industry goods area where considerable production overcapacity exists.

The long-term sourcing commitments being now undertaken by western exporters as a result of CA obligations in third world countries will result in some production shifts toward selected developing countries in the light and bulk commodity industries as well as in processing and assembly within labor-intensive industrial sectors.

The need to accommodate special political relations with third world countries, or to support major project commitments assumed by western firms abroad, creates the potential for western government involvement with selected CAs.

In future years, some developing countries with large populations may see fit to use CA obligations assumed by a foreign exporter as a means to address local employment requirements or those for social development, besides the traditional need to generate foreign exchange. CA-related investment of resources in these sectors, although not directly affecting the country's balance of trade and payments, would be designed to create jobs through emphasis on labor-intensive projects or to improve health and other public sector services of the purchasing country. In the present unstable environment in many populous third world nations, where political instabilities breed on economic ones, defusing socially motivated pressures may well become adequate compensation for the loss of foreign exchange revenue.

chapter

2

Compensatory Arrangements and Official Attitudes

Bilateralism for commercial purposes is a practice inconsistent with the principles fostering a multilateral system of trade and payments to which the General Agreement on Tariffs and Trade (GATT) and the International Monetary Fund (IMF) subscribe.[1] Although the emer-

[1]The General Agreement on Tariffs and Trade, signed on October 30, 1947, and entered into force on January 1, 1948, is a multilateral agreement subscribed to by 87 governments accounting for four-fifths of world trade. It is the only multilateral agreement that sets agreed rules for international trade which aim to liberalize world commerce. The International Monetary Fund's Articles of Agreement entered

gence and proliferation of CAs were not envisaged at the time of the drawing up of the charters on which the GATT and the IMF are founded, the implications of coercion, market foreclosure, and restrictions on payment transfers inherent in CAs have now focused renewed official attention on such arrangements. In this chapter we shall identify and outline the main CA-related attitudes and concerns of international organizations and developed and developing countries, leaving to more versed experts the task of justifying the validity of the concerns raised.

GATT, the IMF, and OECD Attitudes

When the GATT negotiators set about to reshape the international trade system after World War II, they set as an objective the establishment of a framework of rules which would allow international trade to be conducted on a nondiscriminatory basis, would afford protection of domestic industries through custom tariffs rather than other commercial measures, and would eliminate quantitative restrictions such as unilateral import quotas. The resulting GATT clauses allow escape provisions and waivers under certain defined circumstances, whenever a member country's economic or trade conditions so warrant, but require that the member help clarify difficulties and find equitable solutions to his problems through consultations with the other members concerned.

The General Agreement's fundamental objection to all bilateral arrangements including CAs is that by their nature, they undermine the GATT's basic principles of nondiscrimination and general prohibition of quantitative restrictions. Addressing the former principle, the General Agreement restricts bilateral arrangements between an importing and an exporting country which are discriminatory to other trading parties; addressing the latter, it prohibits all measures, including quotas and import-export licenses, that would restrict commercial flows between trading parties. While providing certain conditions for waivers, the GATT's articles are silent about consensual arrangements whereby the exporting country agrees to the discriminatory measures imposed on its exports.

into force on December 27, 1945. The Fund was established to provide a machinery for consultation and collaboration among signatory members on international monetary problems.

As a result, many countries have found it expedient to bypass the safeguard clauses within the General Agreement in favor of informal bilateral arrangements resulting in trade restrictions, in order to avoid the conditions imposed by the waivers. The latter require nondiscriminatory application of any restrictions among all foreign import sources as well as consultations with, and compensation of, any exporting countries affected by the restrictions. In the changed international trade environment since the mid-1970s, bilateral arrangements covering textiles, steel, automobiles, ships, and consumer electronics are once again proliferating in world trade, even gaining a measure of legitimacy through their unchallenged acceptance.

While unilateral import quotas, which were common before World War II, have been largely removed from international trade because of the GATT, protectionism and bilateralism are again creeping into world trade under new forms which the GATT articles do not explicitly address. In the case of CAs, while these arrangements may not be illegal according to the wording of the GATT articles, their consequences flout the spirit of the open, market-driven, multilateral trading system which is the basic reason for the General Agreement's existence. It must also be remembered that the GATT articles are intended to regulate the conduct of member governments and not that of the countries' individual businesses. Because only two GATT member countries, Romania and Indonesia, have at this writing mandated countertrade by law, while other members (about 25 countries) practice some forms of CAs under internal administrative regulations or have enacted enabling legislation (e.g., Mexico), the applicability of existing GATT clauses to such activities may be controversial unless it can be established that specific rules of the General Agreement are being contravened.

In the absence of a GATT waiver, government-inspired impositions of countertrade measures on foreign exporters may be interpreted as contravening Article XI of the General Agreement, which prohibits import restrictions other than tariff duties. Restrictions imposed by importers on outlet markets where countertrade goods and services may be disposed of by exporters could also be challenged under Article XI as a quantitative trade restriction. Mandated domestic-content requirements imposed by CAs also appear to contravene the letter of Article III which bans restrictions "relating to the . . . use of products in specified amount or proportion . . . which . . . must be supplied from domestic sources." In practice, a consensual arrangement in which the exporting country agrees to abide by the restrictions imposed by the importing country precludes in all likelihood a viable challenge to the restrictions under GATT rules.

The IMF's policy to promote a multilateral system of international payments has resulted in consistent pressure by the Fund on its members to reduce reliance on bilateral payment agreements. The IMF's particular concern with CAs stems from fears of potential restrictions by such practices on payments and transfers for international transactions. These include restrictive and discriminatory payments or exchange practices by governments, such as impositions of CA-related penalties or other costs, blocking of payments, or contractual impositions on exporters to accept payments in the importer's domestic currency whenever such payments are tied to conditions restricting purchases of counterdeliveries in the importing country. It could be argued that by conditioning balance-of-payments financing to requirements that a country bring its foreign trade in parity (i.e., by enhancing exports and reducing imports), the Fund is fostering countertrade initiatives intended to achieve such a goal. As in the case of the GATT, the Fund's jurisdiction and retaliatory powers extend only to government activities, both direct and indirect, and not to the activities of private firms.

Mandatory countertrade arrangements in east-west trade have been opposed on economic and trade-policy grounds by both the Organization for Economic Cooperation and Development (OECD) and the United Nations Commission for Europe.[2] The issue of east-west countertrade, which has resulted in numerous OECD studies,[3] continues to be debated.

The U.S. Government's Attitude

A long-standing objective of U.S. trade and monetary policy during the post–World War II years has been the development of an open, nondiscriminatory, and multilateral trading system which avoids restrictive trade practices such as CAs. The U.S. government's limited assistance provided to U.S. exporters involved in CAs reflects this

[2]The Organization for Economic Cooperation and Development was set up in December 1960 to promote policies designed to achieve economic growth in its 24 member countries, the industrialized economies, as well as in nonmember countries, on a multilateral, nondiscriminatory basis.

[3]See, for example, *East-West Trade; Recent Developments in Countertrade,* OECD, Paris, 1981.

attitude. But on a few occasions in the past, the U.S. government's export credit agency, the Export-Import Bank, did extend credit to exports involving compensatory transactions, and the U.S. Department of Commerce export support programs do include advisory assistance to exporters faced with compensatory obligations.

Today the pressure on the U.S. government to aid American exporters' interests abroad is increasing. The proliferation of CAs in international trade is creating a dilemma for the U.S. government, torn between its long-standing policy objectives of multilateralism and its pragmatic desire to expand foreign trade. While clearly opposed to government-mandated countertrade impositions and not encouraging its exporters to engage in the practice, the U.S. government seems content not to interfere with the private sector's market decisions to involve itself with CAs, except when national security considerations are at stake.

U.S. federal agencies are aware that they might be requested in the years ahead to provide guidance and assistance to domestic industrial projects in the developing countries, such as the development of hydro resources in the People's Republic of China, which will likely entail sizable CAs and long-term commitments of resources on the part of U.S. firms. Thus, the companies will expect active sponsorship by their government on behalf of such projects (e.g., support and promotion at government-to-government level, officially backed loans and political-risk guarantees, and trade and investment treaties) if they are to hazard prolonged involvement in potentially unstable areas of the world and accept protracted returns on the investment of their resources. In response to CA-related pressures by exporters, several western governments have opted to sanction quasi-private organizations to assist their companies with CAs. These will be described in the next section of this chapter.

Whether the U.S. government might adopt a similar initiative is unclear and unlikely at the present. Instead, the U.S. government has relied on legislation to provide American business with new tools which, depending on their exploitation by the exporter, could help him to penetrate or expand markets abroad. One such legislation is the Export Trading Company Act of 1982. The legislation is intended to stimulate export initiatives, particularly of small and medium-sized firms, by liberalizing restrictions on investment by banks in export trading companies and by allowing exemption from antitrust law for the exporting trading company's member firms. Although specifically intended to foster U.S. exports, the act's antitrust provision could potentially facilitate the handling of countertrade obligations assumed by member companies, through the allocation of counterdeliveries among the consortium's members on a credit-and-debit basis (see discussion in Chapter 10).

Western Government Attitudes

Support of CAs by the industrialized countries of western Europe and by Japan has been facilitated by these countries' export policies which in many instances are more liberal than those of the United States. These export-development programs include favorable tax and credit terms as well as nontax incentives (e.g., investment and interest subsidies and grants) and insurance assistance (e.g., against inflation and exchange rate fluctuations) which are either not available to the American exporter or seldom matched in the United States.

In France, West Germany, and Japan, resource policies provide for the extension of special loans, government-supported guarantees, and insurances as well as grants for exploration and/or development of specified strategic mineral projects in specified geographic areas, provided that the projects commit part of their output to the western country.[4] These programs are intended to promote the participation of the countries' companies in the projects as well as to ensure access to the resulting raw material resources. France extends low-interest development loans to projects in the franc-zone countries and has provided mixed export credits to non-franc-zone countries on the condition that part of the projects' resultant production is committed to France. An example is the French government export-credit extension to India in 1981 for an alumina-aluminum complex, part of whose output is exported to France.[5] Japan's International Cooperative Agency provides grants for capital projects undertaken by Japanese companies abroad with the participation of the host government. Low-interest loans are also provided by the Japanese Overseas Economic Development Fund for "national projects" ensuring long-term access to the projects' output. Similarly, West Germany's resource-development program provides favorable credits to resource-exploitation projects, such as the development of a Brazilian iron ore mining project contracted in 1976.

[4]P. C. F. Crowson, "The National Mineral Policies of Germany, France, and Japan," *Mining Magazine,* June 1980, p. 252.

[5]"Aluminum Plant Planned by India, Pechiney Unit," *Wall Street Journal,* Jan. 12, 1980, p. 23.

Often CAs are undertaken under government-negotiated bilateral "economic agreements" which provide for exchanges of natural, technological, and capital resources. For example, Japan has negotiated for Mexican oil imports paid for by Japanese exports. As a result, The Mexican Petroleum Import Co., Ltd., was formed in 1980 and La Organizacion Promotora de Conversiones Japan-Mexico was organized in Mexico that same year. Japanese export trading companies, which today account for about two-thirds of Japan's exports, also handle CAs routinely.

Assistance related to CAs and provided by public or private entities in western Europe varies from the advisory services provided by the United Kingdom's Export Policy Branch of the Department of Trade and by national trade associations in West Germany and Belgium, to the commercial-type companies such as Finland's Metex, which represents private and public sector engineering firms and handles its members' and other firms' CAs. In West Germany, CA-related assistance to German firms is provided by the Internationales Zentrum fur Ost-West Kooperation. The Center was established in 1976 as a private institution by the Central Association of German Chambers of Industry and Commerce, the Confederation of German Industry, the Berlin Chamber of Industry and Commerce, and the Berlin Marketing Council.

In Austria, the Liaison Office of Foreign Trade (Evidenzburo), originally created in 1968 as a nonprofit organization to promote its members' east-west trade, is increasingly becoming engaged in the CAs of its membership. Evidenzburo operates under the auspices of the Austrian Federal Chamber of Commerce, the Ministry of Trade, and the Austrian Association of Industrialists on behalf of its dues-paying Austrian and foreign membership, and it tends to concentrate on the product ranges of counterdeliveries that can be absorbed by its members or other Austrian firms.

The French service for CAs was formed in late 1977, with the support of the Ministry of Foreign Trade, by four national trade and industry groups and five banks, with the specific purpose of developing a national capacity for dealing with worldwide CAs incurred by French exporters. Known under the acronym of ACECO (Association pour la Compensation des Exchanges Commerciaux), this semiofficial nonprofit body serves in an advisory capacity to French public authorities and private firms. Under its statutes, ACECO cannot become involved in the implementation of CAs or advise foreign companies. It concentrates its activities on translating the experience gained in CAs into guidance for French exporters, on identifying trading companies or importers willing to assist with such obligations undertaken by its dues-paying members, and on advising competent government authorities on desired policy initiatives that would facilitate exports involving compensatory commitments.

Developing Countries' Attitudes

Enforcement of CAs by developing countries has been traditionally associated with the communist countries' trade practices. In reality, CAs contracted under government-to-government agreements have been a rather common, although not prevalent, practice in the trade among developing countries. Such official arrangements, to be described in the next chapter, include bilateral clearing agreements involving settlements for the traded goods in accounting units denominated in U.S. dollars or other currencies (e.g., Brazil and Romania), barter trade protocols involving direct exchanges of goods (e.g., Bangladesh and the People's Republic of China), or regional trade agreements involving preferential trade and payments terms (e.g., Brazil and Venezuela).

Where developing countries, other than perhaps the Soviet-bloc countries, lack both experience and expertise is in facilitating and promoting CAs which are not government to government but occur between domestic and western firms. At issue are considerations such as understanding and attempting to accommodate commercial rather than political interests; establishing the necessary bureaucratic structure, administrative and policy guidelines, and approval processes to facilitate tie-ins on a routine basis between imports and exports related to CAs; overcoming currency-exchange restrictions arising in such transactions; and, possibly, creating fiscal or other incentives which would encourage domestic manufacturers in the developing country to participate in each other's CAs, thereby allowing the foreign firm a wider choice of compensatory goods and services. The complexities involved in formulating a national policy for CAs, which will treat the practice as a tool of long-range economic planning intended to redress trade and payments imbalances and to address social or sectorial economic needs, may require in future years specialized assistance in the form of compensatory-management services along the lines of the more established asset- and liability-management services provided by major investment bankers.

Indeed, across-the-board and undiscriminated impositions of compensatory obligations on foreign exporters have not fared well in the past. For example, Indonesia's counterpurchase policy implemented in December 1981 has met with wide opposition from western exporters because of its rigid terms and blanket impositions across all types of government-procurement imports. Expected originally to affect contracts worth as much as $4.5 billion a year, the figure has since been revised downward. During 1982 the policy has not met with expected success, accounting for contracts worth less than $300 million. Similarly, many western exporters have forgone doing business with Romania because of the country's strict CA policies affecting all sectors of the economy.

Other developing countries are making use of compensatory practices to suit current economic predicaments and particular goals. Intents may range from modernization of a country's industrial production, as in the People's Republic of China, which is saddled with 350,000 small and medium-sized obsolescent industrial enterprises, to compensation for slumping exports in the face of declining demand, as in Iraq and Qatar, which are paying part of their plant-construction costs in crude oil quoted at cartel prices. Government initiatives fostering CAs also vary, ranging from incentives such as rebates of import tariff duty in the People's Republic of China and discounts for commodity exports in Jamaica, to export impositions on foreign imports and investment, such as export-performance requirements in Mexico and domestic-content requirements in Brazil.

Foreign debt, shortage of capital, and socioeconomic pressures resulting from annual population growth are forcing developing countries to walk a tightrope. Many third world countries realize that even with world recovery, their economies will probably never grow at the boom rates of past decades, and the problem facing their governments becomes how to use to best advantage the leverages provided by the import prospects of their domestic markets and by the western companies' need to compete in export markets. Resulting government-sponsored initiatives must account for the severe import restrictions imposed by the IMF and by western banks as a condition for debt rescheduling, must continue to protect parts of the national markets for domestic companies in industrial sectors such as the automotive and computer ones, and must be able to attract foreign capital and technology. It is obvious why compensatory practices appear to be convenient, low-risk, and immediately enforceable approaches which could achieve the above goals.

Ultimately and with additional experience under the belt, it will become apparent to these countries that developing the capital and technology infrastructure necessary to keep pace with the changing needs in export markets can be helped along by compromising on present restrictive policies which discourage foreign investment by multinationals. Multinationals are among the best-suited exporters with the staying power and resources necessary to weather the current economic predicament in third world markets. The success of present economic readjustments in third world countries, involving shifts from the development of capital-intensive and natural resource projects to job-creating manufacturing and export diversifications (e.g., development of nontraditional exports), will depend to a great extent on the ability of these countries to secure long-term commitments of foreign investment to supplement CA schemes. On their part, the foreign companies' perceptions of long-term risks will be influenced by the ability of developing countries to act with dispatch and to clear bureaucratic and attitudinal bottlenecks which discourage foreign involvement in third world economies.

chapter

3 Forms of Compensatory Trade

As practiced in today's international trade environment, CAs consist of continuously evolving techniques whose forms of implementation are designed, sometimes creatively, to match specific needs and contingencies of the contracting parties. The nomenclature of CA forms has not been uniform or consistent. Not only are similar forms of CAs referred to by different names in the business community, but the terminology traditionally associated with long-standing practices in east-west trade may not suit arrangements evolving in other world markets.

As defined in this text, a CA refers to any contractual commitment imposed as a condition of purchase, by the importer on the exporter, with the intention of creating quid pro quo benefits for the former. These benefits could be derived from trade-related cash flows generated by the exporter on account of the importer, or may result from resource transfers (e.g., technology or capital) from the exporter to the importer which enhance the latter's employment or improve his industrial productivity and sophistication, whether or not exports are involved. Benefits may offset partially the value of the original import, match it, or exceed its value over a span of years.

Creative marketing and financing approaches may be needed in structuring a CA whenever conditions require circumventing import or exchange restrictions, supporting commodity price levels, or making use of services provided by the importer. A single transaction may, depending on its value and size, involve more than one form of CA, although complexity can result in additional unforeseen problems and costs. As indicated earlier, CAs can be transacted under contract between two commercial enterprises, either on their own initiative or in accordance with official directives, or they may be conducted under government-to-government bilateral agreements.

When CAs result in exchanges of goods and services between two parties in different countries, the transactions are known as countertrade or barter, respectively, according to whether financial counterflows are involved or not. Table 1 illustrates types of CAs and applicable terminology for each type of agreement. These are described in detail in the next sections.

Barter

Classically defined, a barter transaction is the straight exchange of goods having offsetting values without any flow of cash taking place. The exchange of goods is usually set out in a single contract between two trading parties, and the terms of the contract are fulfilled without intervention of third parties. Barter agreements are rare in international trade. Commodity traders may swap deliveries of equivalent products to each other's clients around the world, in order to save on transportation costs. For example, Mexico may ship its crude oil to Cuba on Soviet account, in return for Soviet oil shipments to Mexico's customers in Greece.

On occasion a western exporter may find it necessary to enter into a barter arrangement with a foreign customer whenever western export credits are unavailable to finance the transaction. In 1983 General Electric renegotiated its $150 million contract signed 2 years

Table 1
Compensatory Arrangements

Transaction Description	Government to Government	Company to Government Agency	Company to Company
	Forms of Agreements		
Exchanges of goods; no cash flows	Barter agreement		Swap contract
Exchanges of goods; only imbalances settled in cash	Bilateral clearing agreement		
Exchanges of goods; parallel and separate cash flows for imports and exports	Bilateral trade agreement or protocol	Countertrade contract Evidence account	Countertrade contract
Import approval tied to production and technology transfers to importing country* or to export performance	Coproduction license (involving advanced technology transfer)	Domestic content contract Subcontracting Investment performance (foreign investment tied to export performance)	Coproduction Licensing contract Investment performance

*These CAs, combined with contractual provisions for countertrade, are also known as *offsets* and find application in military and high-dollar-value contracts. Offsets are described in Chapter 4.

earlier with Romania, which involved the supply of steam turbines in conjunction with the sale of Canadian nuclear reactors to that country. Under the new terms, General Electric agreed to receive 50 percent of its payments as barter of Romanian goods and 50 percent in cash.

Barter arrangements are also found in the trade between countries under government-to-government agreements. The practice finds application when the countries' trade is governed by political considerations, especially when one of the trading countries is in economic difficulty, lacking the monetary resources to finance its own portion of the parallel import-export transaction. For example, Bangladesh has barter agreements with Pakistan, North Korea, Czechoslovakia, Poland, Romania, Bulgaria, and the People's Republic of China. Under annual arrangements, Bangladesh exports agricultural commodities, textiles, hides, paper products, and other goods to these countries in return for industrial equipment and machinery, chemicals, fertilizers, metals, and medicines. Figure 3.1 illustrates schematically a barter transaction.

Barter trade exchanges have been a growing industry in the United States and Canada. There are about 300 in the two countries, which serve collectively about 100,000 members, mostly small businesses and professionals. Membership is open to domestic as well as foreign companies or individuals. Some U.S. barter exchanges have been recently looking into expanding their activities overseas.

A barter exchange serves as a clearinghouse for the sale and purchase, on either a full barter basis or a part-cash, part-barter basis, of goods and services belonging to its membership. Receivables due in goods and services are denominated in units of account known as trade units or trade credits. These units are credited to one account and debited from another in each transaction, thanks to a computer-assisted network that allows 24-hour access to trading information. Barter exchanges earn their income from annual membership fees and commissions on the gross amount of each transaction.

Bartered goods and services include business services, air travel, hotel accommodations, advertising, insurance, medical care, office space, and unsold inventories of raw materials, equipment, machinery, and consumer products. The barter exchanges' annual trade volumes in the United States are estimated at several hundred million dollars. A few American airline carriers have used the practice for much-needed advertising, following the 1980 Civil Aeronautics Board decision to permit airlines to exchange their seats for goods and services. Major U.S. corporations also conduct barter operations among business units within their own company, as well as with other companies.

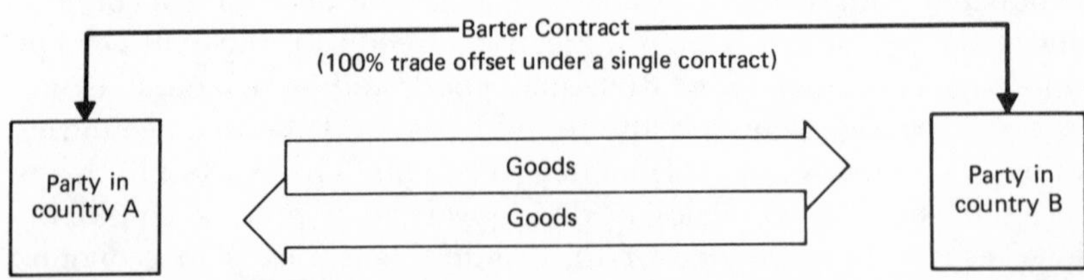

Figure 3.1. Model of a barter transaction.

Countertrade

When reciprocal and contingent exchanges of goods and services are specified by contract and each flow of deliveries is valued and settled in monetary units, the CA is known as countertrade.

Countertrade transactions may be settled under a single contract or under two parallel contracts setting out conditions for imports and exports as well as their linkage. The latter approach is more widely used in international trade because it provides the flexibility of separate financing, guarantees, and payments. It also facilitates the intervention of third parties to whom the primary exporter may transfer his purchase commitments, or parties who may assume the obligation to export on account of the primary importer. Countertrade contracts specify the percentage of the import value to be offset by counterdeliveries. This *countertrade ratio* can be a fraction of, equal to, or more than the value of the imports.

The motivations behind countertrade impositions by importers may be the latter's urge to market abroad goods in low demand or goods for which no adequate marketing support is available; the need to finance imports for which insufficient or no allocations have been budgeted; or the desire to upgrade production processes and utilize excess production capacity under long-term export contracts. Several types of countertrade forms practiced in international trade are outlined below.

Direct compensation (or buyback), whereby the counterdeliveries are resultant from and related to the original export.

Indirect compensation (or counterpurchase), whereby the counterdeliveries are not derived from or related to the original export.

Reverse countertrade (or junktim), whereby anticipatory purchases by an exporter are contractually qualified for credit to be offset against his subsequent sales. Such credits can be made transferable to third parties.

Direct-compensation arrangements may involve capital projects erected with western-supplied technology, capital, and equipment, for which the western contractor obliges himself to market a portion of the project's output. Fulfillment of direct-compensation obligations generally takes place over 5 to 10 years, with the cumulative value of western purchases over the lifetime of the contract often exceeding the value of the original export contract. Figure 3.2 shows a diagram of a typical direct-compensation transaction.

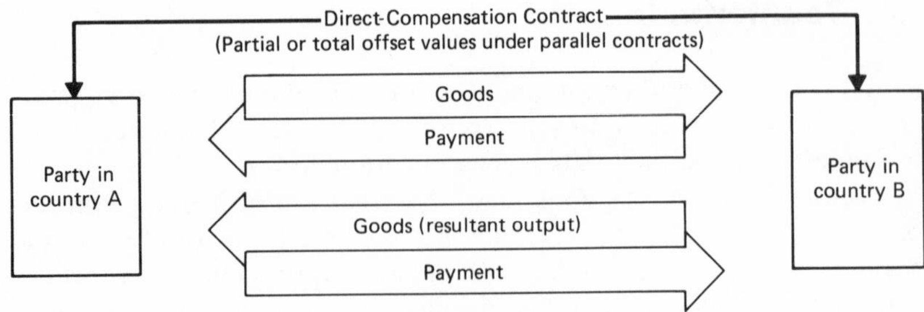

Figure 3.2. Model of a direct-compensation transaction.

Examples of direct-compensation agreements are especially abundant in the communist countries. For example, the West German company Salzgitter has sold low-density polyethylene plants to the Soviet Union for resultant products; the French company Creusot-Loire and, separately, the Italian company Montedison have installed ammonia plants in the Soviet Union and are now receiving ammonia deliveries as repayment; the U.S. firm Steiger sold technology and equipment for manufacturing tractors to Hungary and agreed to buy back tractor axles from the Hungarian plant it equipped. The People's Republic of China is actively engaging these days in compensation arrangements for the manufacture of light industrial products (e.g., garments, plastic goods, processed food, appliances); the arrangements involve processing and assembly of products in China, using know-how, raw materials, components, and machinery supplied by the foreign party.

In some developing countries direct-compensation arrangements involve production-sharing ventures in the extraction and processing of mineral ores, with outputs shared among the investors. Examples include a Brazilian-Japanese venture for production of bauxite in Brazil, a French-British-Australian venture for aluminum production in Australia, a West German–Philippine venture for iron ore extraction in the Philippines, and a Japanese-Peruvian venture for copper ore extraction and production of concentrates in Peru.[1] Other direct-compensation arrangements include the construction of a tire plant with equity participation by the French in Brazil and of a nickel smelter by the British in Colombia.

Counterdeliveries under an indirect-compensation arrangement may involve manufactured or semimanufactured goods, raw materials, machinery, or other items which are not related to the primary

[1]James I. Walsh, "The Growth of Develop-for-Import Projects," *Resources Policy,* Butterworth & Co. Publishers, December 1982, p. 277.

export for which they constitute repayment. The value of the counter-deliveries over the lifetime of the contract is generally less than 100 percent of the primary export contract value, except in countries like Indonesia where full offset for imports are required for government procurements. Because of different contract maturities related to the exchange of goods, it is preferred practice to execute indirect-compensation transactions under two parallel contracts. Figure 3.3 illustrates the model for an indirect-compensation transaction.

Examples of indirect-compensation arrangements are also abundant in world trade. A recent Brazilian agreement with Ecuador involves the export of Brazilian electrical and electronic equipment to the Ecuadorian state telecommunications company in return for petroleum imports. Petroleum is also being provided to Japanese contractors in partial payment for plant construction costs by Iraq and Qatar, and to South Korean contractors by Libya and Iraq. Denmark has traded medicines for Honduran coffee, and Danish firms will be importing New Zealand goods over 10 years as a result of an 1982 contract won by a Danish contractor for building a passenger and cargo ferry in New Zealand. In recent years there has been increasing emphasis by governments of developing and some developed countries to link large foreign procurements with transfers of technology. Examples of the latter are the so-called industrial-cooperation policies of Norway and the United Kingdom, which tie access to petroleum

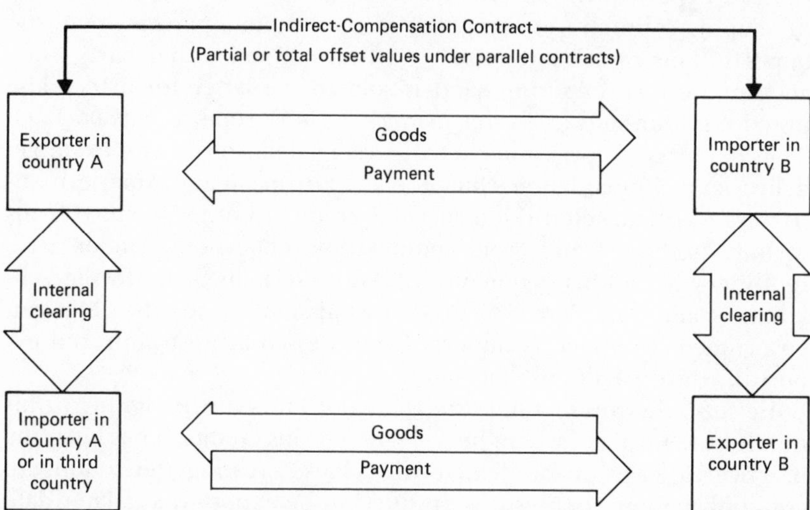

Figure 3.3. Model of an indirect-compensation transaction.

exploration and development of national resources by foreign companies to the contractors' contributions in the area of technology transfer or to subcontracting in the host nations' industries. For example, the United Kingdom government policy requires North Sea petroleum operators to place at least 70 percent of development contracts (such as the construction of offshore drilling platforms) with British manufacturers.

In the Soviet-bloc countries, indirect-compensation arrangements with western firms date back at least to the late 1960s. Such deals usually involve counterdeliveries of foodstuffs, chemicals, industrial products, and machinery. For example, the Austrian firm Chemie Linz has provided fertilizers and pesticides to East Germany for potassium salts and special chemicals. In another example of a counterpurchase transaction, McDonnell Douglas Corporation sold Yugoslavia seven DC-9 airplanes and, in return, agreed to buy tools and canned hams and to act as broker for marketing other Yugoslavian goods in the United States. In the Soviet Union or eastern Europe, the counterdeliveries may be supplied by the state foreign-trade organization which negotiated the import contract or by other such organizations. The latter procedure is known as *countertrade linkage* and requires authorization from appropriate authorities in the country (e.g. the Ministry of Foreign Trade).

Sometimes a western importer of goods from a developing country can negotiate in its import contract a clause by which it is granted the right to export to the seller or, more seldom, to another firm in the developing country, western goods amounting to a percentage of the imports. This right can be made transferable to another party—i.e., another western exporter—and is sold to the latter for a fee. The practice is known as *reverse countertrade* or, in Europe, as *junktim*. Such deals have found application in east-west trade involving, for example, deliveries of Romanian machine tools to European and American importers who marketed the associated credits to other western firms wishing to export and avoid countertrade obligations. Under a recently negotiated arrangement, the West German firm Metallgesellschaft claims to have secured permission from the Mexican government to offset its imports from Mexico against approved exports by third parties to that country.

Because the western importer may not know at the signing of his purchase contract to whom he will later sell his credits, it has been the practice to leave unspecified, in the clause creating the contingent credit obligation, the western products to be exported at a later date and the names of their prospective purchasers in the developing country. The vagueness has created problems for western exporters trying to qualify the acquired credits and have them accepted as substitution for countertrade obligations. As a result, some western importers negotiating credit clauses have lined up prospective western exporters early in the negotiating phase and have specified in such clauses the names of the products to be exported by the latter, together with the names of the western exporters and their customers in the developing country.

Under a special variation of anticipatory performance resulting in the exemption of countertrade impositions, a major Austrian bank agreed to finance Ghana's exports to East Germany in return for securing exemption from countertrade for Austrian exports to Ghana.

Evidence Account

Indirect-compensation transactions may sometimes occur under a trade arrangement known as an *evidence account.* Evidence accounts are umbrella trade agreements between a western exporter and a government entity in a developing country (e.g., an industrial ministry or a provincial authority) which are designed to facilitate trade flows when countertrade is a requirement and when the existing trade turnover between the two parties is significant and expected to increase. The agreements require that two-way trade between the western firm, other parties designated by it, and the commercial organizations under the jurisdiction of the developing country's signatory be partially or fully balanced over a specified period of time, typically 1 to 3 years. Characteristics of evidence accounts are:

Individual trade transactions do not need to be offset through counterdeliveries, but cumulative payment turnovers at the end of the specified period have to balance according to the agreement's terms.

Each import or export transaction is settled by cash.

Trade flows are monitored, and financial settlements occur through the developing country's bank of foreign trade and a bank specified by the western signatory to the agreement.

Figure 3.4 illustrates schematically a model evidence account. Because balancing of payments occurs over many transactions, each set-

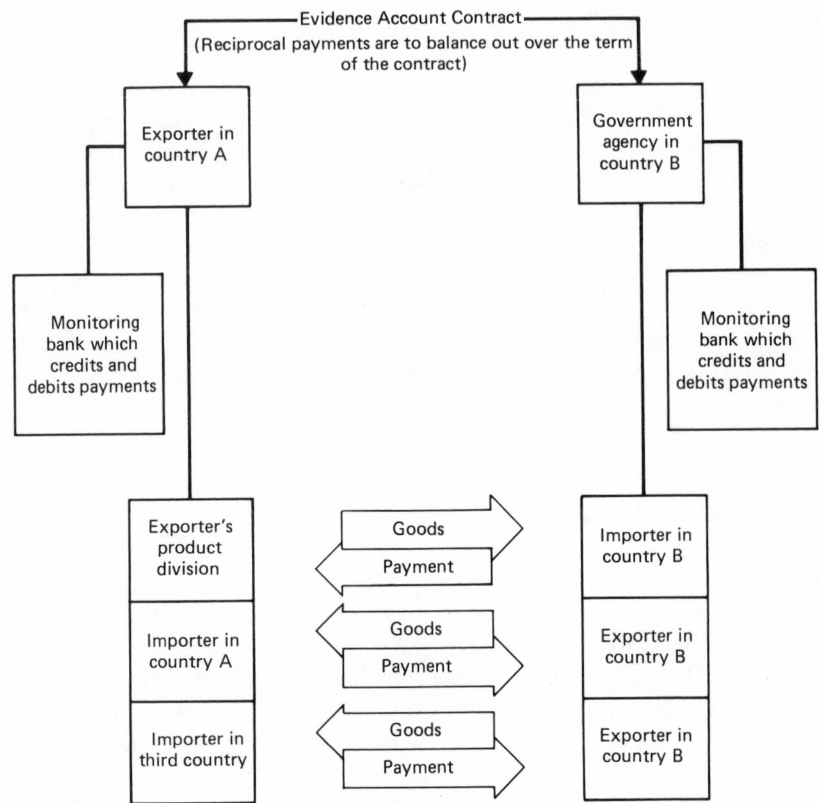

Figure 3.4. Model of an evidence account transaction.

tled in cash, rather than for individual transactions as in the case of countertrade arrangements, evidence accounts hold certain advantages over CAs. A mix of western exporters and importers grouped under the same umbrella agreement, together with a similar mix of firms in the developing country, may allow enough choice to conduct transactions on purely commercial considerations, i.e., avoiding price inflations of exports to compensate for marketing unwanted counterdeliveries or avoiding subsidies to brokers to whom the counterdeliveries are transferred.

Disadvantages associated with evidence accounts are also numerous. These can be attributed to the costs of monitoring individual transactions by the two assigned banks; the difficulties in assembling appropriate exporter and importer mixes on either side whose trading interests match; the lack of incentives for western importers to conduct their trade under the agreement rather than on their own; and the general lack of incentive of participating firms to exceed the annual trade levels set by the agreement terms. Trade under evidence accounts has been practiced in the Soviet-bloc countries and, recently, in the People's Republic of China; the U.S. firm General Motors has signed several such agreements with Chinese industrial ministries, and the British trading house Bowater has an agreement with the Guangdong province.

Bilateral Clearing and Switch

Another form of bilateral compensatory trade is the clearing arrangement by which two governments formally agree to exchange a number of products over a specified period of time, usually 1 year. The agreement specifies the type and volume of products and may additionally list goods or commodities which each side has the option to export to the other for a total agreed value. Conditions regarding the goods' quality, prices, and transportation are agreed upon in individual supply contracts, with exporters in each country being paid by local banks in domestic currencies and the importers crediting the exporters' account—at a designated domestic bank—in a clearing currency that can be used only to buy goods in the importers' country.

The value of the goods traded under the agreement is denominated in *clearing accounting units* expressed in major currencies, e.g., clearing dollars, swiss francs, rupees, or, in the trade within the Soviet-bloc countries, transferable rubles. The agreement requires that all trade exchanges stop beyond a maximum specified trade imbalance, or *swing,* which usually is set at about 30 percent of the yearly trade volume agreed upon. Exchanges of goods are not resumed until additional exports from the country with the trade deficit decrease the imbalance below the level of swing allowed by the bilateral agreement. Such an imbalance, until removed, represents an interest-free credit to one country by the country with the trade surplus. Trade imbalances at the end of the contracted agreement period have to be settled in cash in the specified currency or converted into cash by switching the rights to the trade imbalance to interested third parties at discounted prices. Figure 3.5 illustrates the diagram of a bilateral clearing agreement.

Clearing agreements have decreased in importance and number since the 1950s, as most countries are now conducting their trade in hard currencies. One of the countries still active in bilateral clearing

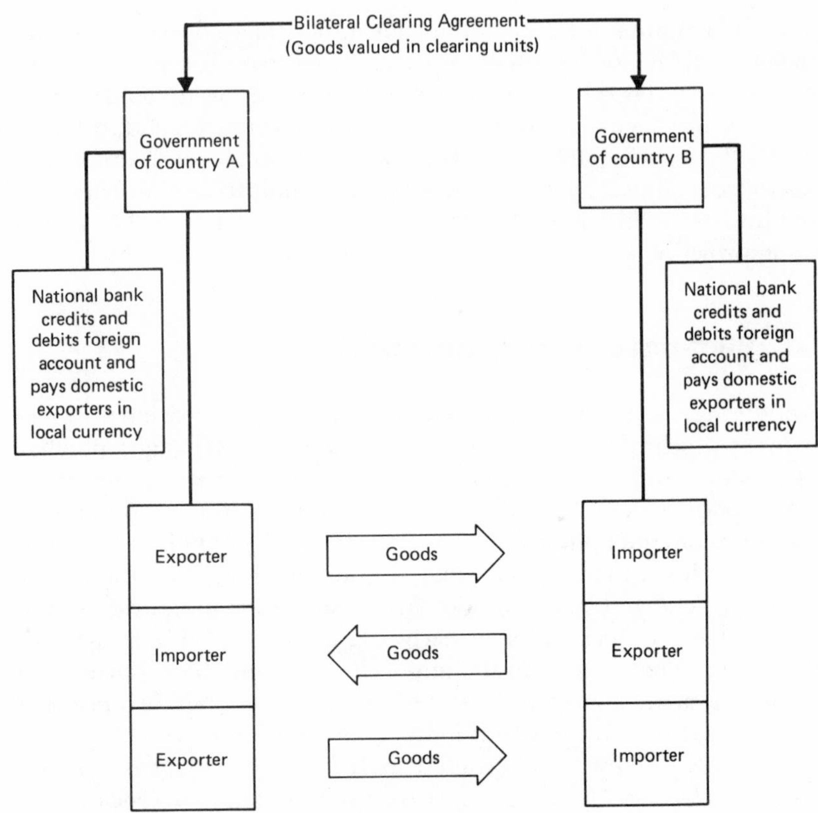

Figure 3.5. Model of a bilateral clearing agreement.

trade is Brazil, which has such agreements with the Soviet-bloc countries. Although a Brazilian importer might not prefer to buy oil-drilling rigs or medical equipment from Romania and Hungary, Brazil's lack of foreign exchange and the political considerations related to fulfilling the bilateral agreement's obligations dictate importing the eastern European goods.

The limitations inherent in clearing agreements have led to the practice of *switching* to third parties the obligation to wipe clean imbalances in bilateral trade. Switch trade is based on the multilateral use of bilateral clearing currencies, and is made possible by a stipulation in a bilateral agreement providing that the country with a surplus in bilateral trade could make available to a third party a portion or all of its clearing account. The third party which acquires rights to the clearing-account surplus purchases goods from the country having a clearing-account deficit. Through a series of complex international transactions that could include barter, the third party converts these goods into hard currency.

The prices of goods transferred to third parties are substantially discounted from the nominal values assigned to them in the clearing agreement. Trading houses that specialize in switch dealings are instrumental in concluding these complex transactions. Western firms and trading houses have used the clearing agreements between certain communist and developing countries to trade with either the communist or the developing countries. For example, U.S. medicines and European-made components for Rank-Xerox copier machines manufactured in India have been shipped to the Soviet Union through the Indo-Soviet clearing agreement, and U.S. fertilizers have been exported to Pakistan through the Romanian-Pakistani agreement. Table 2 lists the bilateral clearing agreements between the Soviet-bloc countries and the third world.

Bilateral Trade Agreements, or Protocols

Some western governments have provided still another vehicle for CAs through the implementation of bilateral trade agreements, or protocols, with developing nations. The agreements, often tied to western credit lines, are intended to preserve or enhance the countries' share of each other's market in one or more economic sectors or to support the development of a major industrial project in the developing country. Under such agreements, Japan has committed itself to build industrial complexes in several Middle Eastern countries in exchange for deliveries of petroleum and is exchanging Japanese industrial goods, technology, and capital for Chinese petroleum and coal exports under a 13-year agreement with the People's Republic of China (1978–1990). Under similar protocols, France and Canada have negotiated for Mexican oil imports paid for by their exports, and Italy has provided Venezuela with technical assistance in the fields of agriculture, agro-industry, and university education, also in exchange for petroleum.

Trade agreements signed by the U.S. government with developing countries (e.g., the People's Republic of China) have not been project-oriented or specific as to the nature of the goods to be exchanged; rather, they have been a trade-enabling vehicle providing a framework for general economic and commercial relations. Because the agreements rely on the free will of the two countries' exporters to engage

Table 2
Bilateral Clearing Agreements between Soviet-Bloc Countries* and the Third World in 1983

	Albania	Bulgaria	Cuba	Czechoslovakia	E. Germany (GDR)	Hungary	Poland	Romania	U.S.S.R.
Afghanistan				•					•
Algeria	•								•
Bangladesh		•		•	•	•	•	•	•
Brazil		•			•	•	•	•	
People's Rep. of China	•	•	•	•	•	•	•	•	•
Colombia		•			•	•	•	•	
Costa Rica							•		
Ecuador			•		•	•	•	•	
Egypt									•
Finland		•			•	•			•
Ghana								•	
India				•	•		•	•	•
Iran	•	•		•	•	•	•	•	•

*Clearing agreements among Soviet-bloc countries are conducted in transferable rubles.

†Clearing agreements cover specified commodities.

Table 2
Bilateral Clearing Agreements between Soviet-Bloc Countries* and the Third World in 1982 (*Continued*)

	Albania	Bulgaria	Cuba	Czechoslovakia	E. Germany (GDR)	Hungary	Poland	Romania	U.S.S.R.
Lebanon				•			•		
Mali									•
Mexico			•						
Nepal		•					•		•
Pakistan†		•		•		•	•		•
São Tomé and Principe					•				
Somalia									•
Syria									•
Venezuela			•						
Yugoslavia	•			•	•				•

*Clearing agreements among Soviet-bloc countries are conducted in transferable rubles.

†Clearing agreements cover specified commodities.

in mutually beneficial trade, and do not specify either the nature of the goods and quantities to be traded or the conditions, such agreements cannot be considered compensatory trade.

Domestic Content

Domestic-content requirements are government-mandated regulations calling on foreign companies to perform locally a specified portion of the work contracted on a project or product. The aim of the requirements is to create domestic jobs, improve industrial sophistication through technology transfers, and reduce payment transfers to foreign contractors through the leverage provided by rights of the imports. Thus, domestic-content impositions qualify as CAs.

Domestic-content programs may be designed to protect a specific industrial sector from foreign imports, as is the intent of proposed legislation affecting U.S. automotive production, or may apply to government procurement contracts as administrative regulations, as is more common. In the latter case, the regulations will allow foreign contractors the option to satisfy the requirements through local purchases along with domestic manufacturing. Several countries have established domestic-content requirements for foreign procurements, and others may follow suit.

In Australia, government policy requires that government-funded or publicly funded purchases of equipment and services of high overseas content (e.g., aircraft, computers, transportation and telecommunication equipment) be subject to compensatory provisions amounting to 30 percent and up. Any domestic participation proposals by the foreign supplier need to include commitments to purchase Australian goods or may involve local manufacturing of components. The government makes special allowances for technology-transfer provisions that will benefit its industry. The regulations are enforced under the Australian Offsets Program, a civilian program relating to nonmilitary procurements, and the Australian Industry Participation Program, which governs military purchases. Since May 1982, administrative responsibility for the two programs has been assigned to a new Department of Defense Support Office. At present, new guidelines are being studied whereby Australian resource-development projects contracted by foreign companies will also require "adequate participation" by Australian consulting engineering firms.

All New Zealand government tenders exceeding NZ$2 million in value have included in the last years an optional requirement to purchase for export local goods or, if feasible, to contract for domestic manufacture a portion of the project or of any other product. The actual value proposed for any CA is decided by the foreign supplier and reflects the competitiveness of the situation. The New Zealand Department of Trade and Industry evaluates the tenders selected by the domestic purchaser and monitors resulting CA sales periodically. In December 1982 the government introduced new regulations requiring a minimum 30 percent mandatory participation, measured in terms of man-hours, by New Zealand professional service organizations in all major projects requiring government approval. The regulations apply to feasibility and planning studies, project design, and design and construction management.

In Israel, administrative regulations require that procurements above $100,000 by government agencies, and by private domestic firms to which government financial assistance is provided, seek clearance from the Israel Industrial Cooperation Authority. The principal functions of this office, which reports to the Ministry of Industry and Trade and is guided by an advisory council of 12 businessmen, is to negotiate for offsets providing for locally manufactured content or counterpurchase arrangements and to supervise compliance with agreed terms. Generally, the offset requirement is for at least 25 percent of the contract and is negotiable on a case-by-case basis. Local content arrangements are preferred over local purchases because of their long-range benefits for the Israeli economy.

Table 3 lists examples of several types of government programs which mandate or abet CAs in specific industrial sectors.

Special Practices

As hard-currency credit is becoming constrained in trade with developing countries, attention is shifting to ways which could make use of soft currencies obtained in payment for western exports. Because of exchange restrictions imposed by developing countries and the unwillingness of many western banks to discount these countries' receivables which are owned by western exporters, the de facto value of any soft-currency payments translates into hard currency only to the degree that it is possible to obtain goods and services in the developing country and market them in hard-currency countries. In recent months, about $20 to $30 million worth of dollar-denominated receivables due American exporters by Mexican companies have been converted into pesos through the services of Metallgesellschaft Services, Inc., a New York–based subsidiary of the West German firm Metallgesellschaft. These pesos were used to purchase exportable Mexican goods at pre-

Table 3
Selected Examples of Government Programs Tied to Compensatory Arrangements

Form	Country	Economic Sector
Government procurement (tied to countertrade)	Israel	All procurements above $100,000; domestic content also an alternative option
	Australia	All major purchases; domestic content also an alternative option
	New Zealand	Most
	Pakistan	Most
	Yugoslavia	Most
	Comecon	Most
	Indonesia	All government procurements in excess of 500 million rupiah ($780,000)
	Canada	Case by case
Investment performance (tied to exports)	Australia	Development of extractive resources
	Morocco	Automotive
	Canada	Case by case
	Greece	Case by case
	South Korea	Case by case
	Brazil	All
	Mexico	All

mium rates, which Metallgesellschaft Services marketed abroad for currencies convertible into U.S. dollars, making the discounted proceeds available to the American firms. Although not a clear-cut CA, the transaction illustrates an option as to how hard-currency debt, in certain circumstances, may be disposed of with appropriate third-party assistance, albeit at a discount. Soft currency derived from partial payments for western exports also has been used on several occasions in defraying local costs incurred by western exporters in Yugoslavia and Latin America.

The procuring of equipment and services in developing countries, in cooperation with a western company's subsidiary or other local firms, is an alternative for western contractors which could minimize hard-currency outlays for major capital projects contracted in third markets. Notwithstanding the difficulties of implementation, this may

Table 3
Selected Examples of Government Programs Tied to Compensatory Arrangements (Continued)

Form	Country	Economic Sector
Domestic-content requirement	Argentina	Automotive
	Brazil	Automotive and electronics
	Australia	Major government procurements
	Israel	Government procurements in excess of $100,000
	Taiwan	Whole-plant procurements by state-owned enterprises
Bilateral trade agreements	Mexico-Brazil	Exchanges specified by agreements
	Mexico-Canada	Exchanges specified by agreements
	Mexico-Japan	Exchanges specified by agreements
	Jamaica-Nigeria	Exchanges specified by agreements
	India-Zambia	Exchanges specified by agreements
	Comecon countries–Bangladesh	Exchanges specified by agreements
	Intra-Comecon clearing agreements	Exchanges specified by agreements

allow the western contractor to share any CA obligations with his partner or to avail himself of the partner's preferential trade arrangements and concessionary export credit terms, such as those extended by Brazil to Nigeria and other African countries. Soviet-bloc countries, which have been involved in several such third-country cooperation projects with western firms, have also in past years provided the services of construction crews to western engineering firms as compensation for plant construction by the western firms in eastern Europe.

chapter 4

The Offset Programs

Compensatory transactions involving military trade and certain civil procurements, such as sales of commercial aircraft, are known as *offsets*. These arrangements usually combine domestic content, coproduction, and technology-transfer requirements with long-term (in excess of 5 years) counterpurchase requirements. Note that "offset" is the name traditionally applied in military trade to CAs as previously defined. Under offset agreements, suppliers such as aircraft makers accumulate credits for efforts that facilitate earnings or savings of foreign exchange for their customers, by means that range from counterpurchases to tourism promotion.

Governments of developed and developing countries alike have been using offset requirements as a tool of industrial development, with benefits often accruing to industrial sectors other than those in which the procurements took place. Thus offset packages, while providing immediate returns to the supplier of military or related equipment, may adversely affect the profits of other industries in the exporter's country. At the same time, offsets enhance the customer's employment and export levels and may result in improvements in the productivity and technical sophistication of his domestic industry.

For example, in 1980 the Canadian government announced that in connection with the $2.3 billion purchase of McDonnell Douglas F-18 fighter aircraft, Canada would benefit from the creation of an estimated 24,000 jobs; participate in the production of aircraft components; receive the necessary advanced manufacturing technologies as well as other transfers in solar energy, cryogenics, health care, and processing of agricultural products; and obtain market-development assistance for Canadian exports and tourism.

Forms of Offset

The characteristics of individual offset arrangements bid under competing export proposals vary considerably from contract to contract and from transaction to transaction. This results from the highly competitive nature of the offset business and the sizable dollar value of related compensatory commitments.

The levels of offset and the complexities of related proposals are designed to anticipate and fulfill various trade, social, and industrial needs of the customer and to reflect the supplier's pressures to forestall competition and expectations to perform. Thus, proposed offset packages may include commercial compensations to alleviate the customer's trade and payment imbalances, may involve direct or indirect investment in depressed industries or regions, or may provide technology transfers intended to benefit designated industrial sectors in the customer's country.

In general, offsets may be grouped in the following types of arrangements:

Countertrade commitments to purchase goods and services from the buyer country. These purchases may involve products and services for civil or defense use and may be undertaken by the supplier himself, his subcontractors, or by third parties for whom the supplier acts as a middleman. Third parties may include government agencies in the supplier's country as well as private sector firms such as brokers and importers. Countertrade credits may also be accumulated by the supplier through any range of initiatives that earn foreign exchange for the buyer country. As a result of Northrop Corporation's sale of F-5 fighter aircraft to Switzerland in 1975, the U.S. company helped find export markets for Swiss products, facilitated Swiss participation in foreign capital projects, and assisted with tourist promotion.

Coproduction, inclusive of assembly, processing, and the manufacture of components or equipment in the buyer's country, based upon transfer of technical information and know-how by the supplier. Overseas production is subject to government-to-government license and involves advanced-technology production or sensitive processes, such as automatic manufacturing technology, metal and composite material processing techniques, and fiber optics systems. Under a 1978 coproduction arrangement involving the manufacture of 100 U.S.–designed F-15s in Japan, Mitsubishi, the program's prime contractor, gained access to technology not previously available in Japan involving the manufacture of composite plastic materials. The technology has proved valuable to Japan's commercial aircraft industry.

Technology transfer, involving production of components and equipment in the buyer's country, under direct contractual arrangement between the supplier and the purchasing government or manufacturer. An example of such a technology transfer is the microwave drying process for agriculture and forestry products proposed for licensing under the 1980 offset package between McDonnell Douglas and the Canadian government. In addition to direct licensed production, the technology transfer may result in research and development programs instituted abroad.

Subcontracting, for compatible components manufactured in the buyer's country. Subcontractor production does not involve transfer of technical information and know-how on the part of the supplier; its main intent is to defray procurement costs and to benefit depressed industrial sectors or production facilities in the buyer's country.

Investment, involving a funding of the operations of a joint company established between the supplier and one or more commercial entities in the buyer's country. Such operations may be commercial in nature or involve research and development programs.

Among the above, countertrade, coproduction, and subcontract production have in the past accounted for the major portion of offset contract value, with technology transfer and foreign investment normally representing less than 10 percent of the value. Coproduction programs are probably the oldest form of offset, dating back to the early 1960s when such arrangements were entered into to assist the sale of DC-9 aircraft to Canada and Italy.

The Role of Governments

Governments play major roles in negotiating or facilitating most offset arrangements. The common roles played by a government in offset transactions are as supplier or facilitator under foreign military sales agreements and as active negotiator or approver of export licenses for coproduction arrangements. Governments may act also as purchasers of products and services from the country exported to and, in some instances, as observers at negotiations. Government intervention and influence, albeit exerted in the interest of exports and national security, may alter the workings of the marketplace. Indeed, commitments assumed under offset arrangements can divert business from firms in the supplier's country and foster the emergence of competitors in the buyer's country.

Coproduction arrangements may also result in increased manufacturing costs, as was the case of the coproduction of F-15s in Japan, while offset requirements by countries such as Canada, which exceed sale values by an average of 20 percent, will result in heavy burdens for the supplier. On occasion, the foreign buyer can profit from the multiplicity of suppliers available to him, especially in a market like that of the United States which thrives on competition. The multiplicity of sources allows the buyer to impose acceptance of large offset commitments on competing suppliers, as these vie against each other by bidding up their offset obligations.

U.S. government policies during the last two decades have advocated a sharing of technology with NATO partners to promote interoperability and standardization in arms production. For this purpose, and in recognition that arms production and trade is a two-way street, the U.S. government has waived under certain circumstances traditional buy-national requirements. Today, U.S. policies to provide large amounts of technology and production know-how to NATO allies as an inducement to purchase U.S. weapons are coming under scrutiny, as official concern is now growing about technology leakage as well as future adverse commercial impacts on U.S. industry. The impact of coproduction programs on U.S. future competitiveness is being studied by several U.S. agencies. U.S. congressional and labor groups, as well as some industry segments, are also becoming aware of and concerned about the problem.

The international framework governing the conduct in trade of commercial aircraft is set forth in the Agreement on Trade in Civil Aircraft. The agreement, which was implemented in U.S. statute by the Trade Agreement Act of 1979, provides for the elimination of tariffs and of nontariff barriers resulting from governmental support of civil aircraft development, production, and marketing. Key provisions of the agreement prohibit "mandatory" coproduction, subcontracting, or technology transfers in conjunction with procurement of civil aircraft, and also forbid the provision of privileges—such as the denial or granting of landing rights—to influence purchasing decisions. In 1981 the United States, France, Britain, and West Germany signed the Common Line Agreement which established a 12 percent interest lending rate for aircraft contracts and a maximum level of government direct-loan participation of 42½ percent of total purchase price. Yet, despite agreements intended to create uniform opportunities in international trade, it is apparent that in today's fiercely competitive export environment, it would be difficult, if not impossible, to rein in and control inducements or concessions to buyers, such as offset commitments offered by private exporters.

Offsets in the Aircraft Industry

Aircraft production and trade is a unique economic sector which, in different countries, relies on various degrees of government backing. This may take the form of easy access to government lending resources or, when necessary, of government support in some direct form. Examples of reputed government intervention range from offers of landing rights to tying airliner sales to military aid.

Like the automotive industry, aircraft manufacturing is highly competitive, capital-intensive, highly leveraged (i.e., bearing a high debt-to-equity ratio), and constantly struggling for survival; unlike most other industries, it relies on highly skilled manpower and advanced technologies. What sets the commercial aircraft production sector apart from the military one, even though the same manufacturer may be in both businesses, is the more difficult path to profitability and the higher risks assumed by the commercial sector. While the military programs enjoy government funding for development and a forecastable market, commercial airplane builders have to rely on guesses regarding future market sizes 10 or 15 years in advance while at the same time accounting for increasing challenges from foreign competition.

Miscalculation can bring losses in the billions of dollars for the company and put the company's net worth and existence on the line. Recent declines in sales of large commercial transport aircraft, as well as of smaller general aviation and helicopter crafts, due to slumping demand for airline services, high interest rates, costs of operation, and a lethargic world economy, may be forcing some aircraft manufacturers to leave the commercial airline business altogether. In today's cutthroat aircraft marketing environment, sales sweeteners such as multimillion-dollar price adjustments or options such as credits for spares, assistance with disposal of old airplanes, and other promotional inducements may be insufficient when faced with the customer's inability to pay or to obtain credit.

The credit squeeze facing airlines, along with pressure on commercial aircraft manufacturers to quickly recoup through sales their multibillion-dollar investments for development and manufacturing, is forcing the industry to accept offsets as a necessary alternative to sale losses and as a competitive edge in marketing. The emergence of the European Airbus Industrie comprising French, British, West German, and Spanish companies, supported by extensive and advantageous export-credit financing, is making U.S. aerospace companies aware of the need to be competitive at all costs, particularly in view of present losses in world market shares. According to a recent report by the Labor-Industry Coalition for International Trade, the U.S. industry's share of all aircraft exports from OECD countries had shrunk from 70 percent in 1975 to 53 percent in 1980. While U.S. civil aircraft exports have been sputtering, orders for U.S. military aircraft have been growing, despite global budget constraints. Yet this sector is also becoming increasingly vulnerable to ever larger offset requirements, as countries find that they can impose such obligations in the present buyer-market environment.

The amount of offset required by purchasing countries has varied from approximately 30 percent (e.g., Switzerland) to over 100 percent (e.g., Canada). Fulfillment of offset obligations may also vary according to the transaction at hand, spanning from 1 to 10 years. It is estimated that offset commitments assumed during the last 10 years by U.S. firms have averaged from \$1 to \$2 billion per year, of which military sales account for over 90 percent of total dollar volume.

In the past, aircraft offset agreements have been on a best-effort basis; that is, they carry no penalty clauses and appear as side letters of agreement to the original export contract, although firm commitments enforced by penalty clauses are becoming the norm today. Subcontractors and supplier companies of the western exporter often are made to participate in the offset obligation of the exporter through a clause in their procurement contracts with the exporter. As annual procurement volume of major aircraft manufacturers runs in the multibillions of dollars and is spread over thousands of suppliers, the manufacturers can exert strong leverage on their suppliers through their buying-power spread.

Offset programs in the aircraft industry are being used both as sales incentives and as marketing tools, and have become an integral element of marketing strategy. Because coproduction arrangements are usually limited by the supplier's government technology-transfer policies and by the purchasing country's industrial and technological base, countertrade requirements are becoming an increasingly important, albeit nowadays difficult to implement, element of offset packages. Countertrade-related export-development initiatives by aircraft suppliers on behalf of their customers are designed to open doors to new markets for the latter through market and product research, through identification of foreign trade partners and business opportunities, and by bringing together prospective buyers and sellers. For example, as a result of McDonnell Douglas's sale of DC-9 aircraft to Yugoslavia, the U.S. company sponsored displays of Yugoslavian products on its premises, to which local buyers were invited. It also organized and led a trade delegation of American businessmen to Yugoslavia on a buying mission. Growing in importance as part of offsets, alongside with countertrade, is the development of tourism programs which are designed to benefit customer countries through the earnings of foreign exchange.

Long-Term Prospects

Civil-aircraft demand is expected to remain sluggish for the next few years, although more than 35 percent of the world's large transport aircrafts are at least 14 years old and will require replacement. On the other hand, the world market for military aircraft over the next decade is forecast to exceed 21,000 units with a value of $196 billion in 1982 dollars. Thus aircraft sales opportunities appear abundant in the future, if financing programs are available to support shipments. Given that economic sluggishness and credit constraints are expected to persist in many world markets, especially those of the third world, innovative approaches to financing aircraft exports will be required in order to allow sales to approach market potentials.

International competition among the world's manufacturers of commercial airplanes, while intensifying, is shifting emphasis from protection of domestic markets against foreign imports to fierce competition for enlisting foreign partners willing to share financial risks and for securing foreign subcontractors. The same practical reasons of survival that apply to the automotive industry suggest that future commercial aircraft will be multinational in components and manufacture. Financing the multibillion-dollar program costs will require capital allocations from several countries or, possibly, the establishment of international pools of financing—such as the international equipment trust proposal developed by the Aerospace Industries Association of America. The proposal would make all worldwide capital markets available for financing commercial aircraft, regardless of origin. Repayment would be guaranteed by government export agencies such as the U.S. Export-Import Bank, and the aircraft itself could represent another form of collateral against payment default.

The extension of concessional terms to aircraft sales under mixed credits, a blend of foreign aid with traditional export financing, could also, if ratified by international agreement, increase the potential of aircraft sales. Finally, refinements in offset programs could facilitate trade opportunities and allow more countries to purchase aircraft, whenever traditional financing is not sufficient or is unavailable to them. Indeed, the credit squeeze affecting growing numbers of prospective clients is forcing some general aviation and helicopter manufacturers to shift the sourcing of export finance from commercial banks to merchant banks, and private financial syndicates, and increasingly to consider compensatory transactions whereby repayment occurs through disposal of counterdelivered goods.

Military and large transport aircraft sales also increasingly rely on offsets for financing exports to both industrialized and developing countries. Because of the sizable dollar value of such transactions, offsets will continue to represent a major portion of the world's countertrade flows. Obligations assumed under offset programs are altering the workings of the marketplace by causing shifts in product sourcing and manufacturing capacity, and by tying down market shares over prolonged periods of time. Given the recent concerns about transfers of advanced technology as part of coproduction, and the limitations inherent to marketing countertrade goods in today's globally depressed markets, it is likely that investment contributions as a share of offsets will grow in future transactions, at least in those countries which already own a diversified industrial base. For example, offset-related investments may involve real estate developments or the customizing of existing manufacturing capacity to the specific requirements of an export market. At any rate, the fulfillment of future offset obligations will require increased sophistication and the services of parties in different professional fields.

In future years, some developing countries with large populations may see fit to emphasize as offsets programs resulting in domestic employment and social development, in addition to the need to generate foreign exchange. Such an approach, although not impacting directly on the country's balance of trade and payments, would be designed to create jobs through emphasis on labor-intensive projects or those intended to improve health and other public sector services of the purchasing country. For such purposes, the large dollar volumes characteristic of offset arrangements are particularly suitable.

chapter 5

Compensation Trade in Commodities

Exchanges involving commodities such as agricultural staple products, minerals, fertilizers, crude oil, bulk chemicals, cement, timber, and others have been common occurrences in international trade. For example, commodity brokers may swap among themselves commodities which they have available in different locations around the globe in order to save on transportation costs; governments may barter their countries' commodities for reasons of need or political interests; exporters of industrial goods and services may counterpurchase commodities, which they market through the services of specialist brokers, to fulfill countertrade obligations.

As part of countertrade arrangements, commodity transactions offer both advantages and disadvantages.

Because of cargo size, a single shipment of commodity counterdeliveries could secure for an exporter a significant portion of his repayment. On the other hand, price volatility and the reluctance of some suppliers to discount market prices of their commodities force western firms to increment export prices in order to absorb costs associated with counterpurchases (e.g., the subsidies to the brokers who will market the commodities). Also, western exports for capital projects contracted by a developing country's industrial ministry may not receive the prompt cooperation from another local ministry under whose jurisdiction the desired compensatory commodities reside, unless appropriate incentives are provided. Except for government-to-government arrangements, where prices of the traded goods are adjusted to offset each other, the issue of any price adjustments may become difficult to settle whenever both legs of a countertrade transaction involve only commodity flows whose prices are pegged to those in the world markets. A possible alternative may be offered in such cases by rebates in transportation and insurance costs.

Government-Sponsored Exchanges

Government-sponsored exchanges involving commodities under barter or protocol arrangements are most common in trade between developing countries. Such arrangements are intended to fulfill domestic supply needs and sometimes to foster political ties, as is the case of the barter arrangements that Vietnam and Bangladesh have with the Soviet Union. Settlements of these transactions usually involve small amounts of cash flows with no interest charges and often benefit from price discounts on the traded commodities. On occasion, a third party may get involved in the bilateral trade exchanges between two countries by supplying his goods on account of one of the signatories to the trade agreement. For example, India obtained crude oil deliveries from the Soviet Union on account of Iran, in fulfillment of the Indo-Iranian trade agreement of 1980. Appendix A lists several examples of commodity exchanges under government-to-government arrangements.

The U.S. Department of Agriculture conducted a barter program from 1950 to 1973. The program was set up to reduce stocks of agricultural commodities acquired through its domestic price-support program by the Commodity Credit Corporation (CCC), the U.S. government's financing organization for American agricultural exports, and to increase the U.S. stockpile of strategic materials. In a second stage from 1963 to 1973, the program was used primarily to procure foreign supplies and services used in projects sponsored abroad by the Agency for International Development and by the Department of Defense.

Authority to barter is vested in the Department of Agriculture by Section 303 of the Agricultural Trade Development and Assistance Act of 1954 (Public Law 480) and the Commodity Credit Corporation Charter Act of 1949.[1] These acts authorize the secretary of the U.S. Department of Agriculture to barter agricultural commodities owned by the CCC for strategic and other critical materials needed for the government stockpile or for foreign-produced supplies and services needed by U.S. agencies operating abroad.

Under the Department of Agriculture barter program, American exporters acquired agricultural products held by the CCC at world market prices and sold them to buyers in countries eligible under the program. The proceeds of the exports were then used to import into the United States raw materials to be transferred to the strategic stockpile. Between March 1950, when CCC cotton was first exchanged for Turkish chrome, and 1967, when the last agreement was signed for the exchange of Australian rutile for cotton and other commodities, approximately 60 strategic materials valued in excess of $1.2 billion were transferred to the strategic stockpile. Between 1963 and 1973, offshore procurements of supplies and services accounted for another $4.8 billion. The program was discontinued as strategic inventories exceeded minimum requirements and CCC-owned inventories were depleted. In February 1982 the Department of Agriculture signed, at the direction of President Reagan, an agreement with the government of Jamaica for the barter of 9115 metric tons of dairy products for 400,000 tons of bauxite to be delivered to the national strategic stockpile (see Appendix B). The total value of the transaction was $13 million. Unlike the previous barter program, these transac-

[1]Other U.S. legislation pertinent to barter is the Foreign Assistance Act of 1974, which authorizes the President of the United States, whenever he determines that it is in the national interest, to furnish assistance, defense articles, or services to a recipient nation in exchange for raw materials. The Strategic and Critical Materials Stockpiling Act of 1979 also gives the President a mandate to "encourage the use of barter in the acquisition of strategic and critical materials."

In March 1982 an interagency working group comprising the departments of Agriculture, State, and Defense, the General Services Administration, and the Federal Emergency Agency was established to review the possibility of reinstating barter as a system to reduce national stockpile deficits through the export of surplus agricultural commodities. Unlike the 1950 Department of Agriculture program, the proposed barter would be under government-to-government agreements.

tions were implemented under a government-to-government agreement. A second barter agreement signed on the same date directed the exchange of 1.2 million tons of Jamaican bauxite for excess U.S. stockpile material and involved a cash remittance to Jamaica.

France, West Germany, and Japan have also instituted CA-like programs to assure stable supplies of essential raw materials for their countries. Their governments provide grants or long-term loans at favorable interest rates, sometimes at longer than average payment periods, for the development of foreign projects which result in the import of specified essential minerals such as alumina, aluminum, bauxite, chromium, copper, iron, magnesium, molybdenum, nickel, and tungsten. In Japan financing is provided by the Overseas Economic Development Fund; in West Germany the financing agency is the Deutsche Gesellschaft fur Wirtschaftliche Zusammenarbeit; and in France, the Banque Francaise du Commerce Exterieur and the Bureau of Geological and Mining Research. By 1984 these countries are expected to have imported, as a result of foreign investments, over 69 million tons of iron and pellets and considerable deliveries of nickel and manganese ore, bauxite, and alumina.[2]

The allocation of investment funds for production-sharing projects by these western governments enhances the opportunities of their exporters to participate in exploration and mining projects abroad, fosters political ties to selected developing countries, secures long-term imports of raw materials needed by their domestic industries, and avoids the inefficiencies of short-term or individual government-to-government barter transactions between developed and developing countries. The latter arrangements—except perhaps for those undertaken between governments of two developing countries—often do not involve discounts on commodity prices; they may result in additional costs because of restrictive requirements specifying the use of the western country's shipping lines, even when it is noncompetitive, and because of inefficiencies in budgetary transfers among the western government's various agencies involved in the transaction.

Exchanges Sponsored by the Private Sector

Commodity trading companies have traditionally imported and exported goods on their own account, operating from the strength of

[2]James I. Walsh, "The Growth of Develop-for-Import Projects," *Resources Policy*, Butterworth & Co. Publishers, December 1982, p. 281.

established market positions or availing themselves of spot-market opportunities. Although their purchases and sales often occur in the same market, these transactions are for the most part independent of each other and thus do not qualify under our definition for CAs. Occasionally, western grain traders have agreed, in support of their exports, to counterpurchase Soviet fertilizer. Nonquota Colombian coffee has been also marketed by traders as compensation for Soviet fertilizer exports. In general, however, the amount of countertrade, as a percent of annual turnover trade of commodity trading houses, has been quite small.

Commodity oversupply and price volatility have contributed to the decline in earnings for many developing nations. Faced with a choice between devaluation and a lowering of prices that would make their commodities more attractive on export markets, an increasing number of developing countries are instead opting to enroll western exporters—through the imposition of CAs—into the brokering ranks alongside trading houses, in the hope of expanding commodity exports and compensating for their lack of foreign exchange. Thus, we see today commodities such as petroleum being offered to western constructor firms by producing countries such as Iran, Iraq, Libya, and others as a means of disposing of surplus inventories at cartel prices; strategic minerals such as cobalt being offered to machinery exporters by Zambia on the condition that it be marketed directly to end users and not through traditional brokerage channels; and agricultural commodities being required as counterpurchases by Indonesia for all government procurements.

Among noncommunist economies, only Indonesia has embraced countertrade under a national program as a tool for export expansion. Because of the rigidity and all-encompassing nature of the country's policy, we shall analyze its scope in more detail in the next section.

Countertrade in Indonesia

Government policy initiatives are usually motivated by reasons which, at the time, may seem compelling. The resulting measures will reflect the degree of understanding of the problem at hand, while the hoped-for results will be limited by the policies' impact on the parties involved. The reasons behind the adoption of countertrade measures by the Indonesian government were multiple and compelling in the early 1980s. The country's nonoil and natural gas exports were dropping, by 10 percent in 1980 and 25 percent in 1981; the oil glut was affecting Indonesia's main earner of foreign exchange; imports and government expenditures were on the increase; and the country was facing a balance of payments which by 1981 had swung from surplus to deficit, at a time when elections were scheduled for May 1982.[3] Having summarily investigated in 1981 the countertrade policies of the Soviet-bloc countries and other transactions such as the Northrop Corporation offset arrangement with the Swiss resulting from the sale of military aircraft, Indonesia decided to adopt the practice for its own use. In this, Indonesia was advised by some major western banks which offered to assist the government with its plans to redress a rapidly deteriorating economic situation.

In January 1982 the Department of Trade and Cooperatives issued its *Guidelines for the Implementation of Linking Government Procurements from Imports with Indonesian Export Products Excluding Petroleum and Natural Gas.* The main provisions can be summarized as follows:

All Indonesian government procurements in excess of 500 million rupiah ($780,000)—with the exception of procurements financed by the World Bank, the Asian Development Bank, and the Islamic Development Bank, as well as the domestic procurement portion of foreign contracts, professional services, and joint venture projects—must be fully offset by exports of Indonesian products other than petroleum and natural gas.

Eligible Indonesian products and exporters are to be identified periodically from a list issued by the Department of Trade and Cooperatives. International prices prevailing at the time of delivery of the Indonesian goods will apply.

Counterpurchases by foreign buyers must be above normal trade levels previously established by them in order to satisfy the countertrade requirement (additionality requirement).

Counterpurchases must be exported to the country of origin of the procurement, unless otherwise allowed by the Indonesian government, and the related contracts must be completed 3 months prior to the completion of the Indonesian procurement.

[3]For a comprehensive discussion on countertrade in Indonesia, see Cathleen E. Maynard, "Indonesia's Countertrade Experience," unpublished paper, November 1983, available from the American Indonesian Chamber of Commerce, Suite 701, 12 E. 41st Street, New York, N.Y., 10017.

The foreign supplier shall be liable to a penalty of 50 percent of the value of any unfulfilled portion of his counterpurchase obligation.

In adopting its countertrade policy with limited evaluation or understanding of potential ramifications, Indonesia was willing to experiment in its foreign trade with a relatively untested practice. This was done on the theory that the global recession had created a buyer's-market trade environment which the country could use to its advantage by shifting marketing risks for the counterdeliveries to western exporters. Also, inspired by the communist countries' policies, Indonesia neglected the fact that the Soviet-bloc countertrade included manufactures and machinery, while Indonesia offered as countertrade mainly primary commodities already subject to international controls such as quotas and other protectionistic safeguard measures. It also chose to disregard the prospect of trade warfare by the other area exporters of agricultural commodities, in the case that Indonesian countertrade-related exports would displace the latter's exports in world markets.

Although Indonesian officials indicated that the new directives could be subject to future modifications if their impact on trade was negative, and that reasonable flexibility would be shown on a case-by-case basis, the stringent wording of the directives forced Indonesian negotiators into a rigid initial negotiating posture, as the directives read more like clauses of a contract rather than flexible guidelines designed to enable a matching of needs through negotiations. The tone of the guidelines, the stiff penalty clause which made insurance coverage necessary, the list of counterpurchases limited to traditional export items, and the inflexibility of Indonesian negotiators trying to abide by the guidelines clauses in order to justify the policy's rationale and to test western reactions all combined to protract negotiations and to increase the reluctance of western exporters to trade with Indonesia. As a result, fewer contracts than expected were signed in the first 12 months, amounting to only about $200 million instead of the $500 million projected for that year. Table 4, released by the Indonesian Ministry of Trade and Cooperatives, lists completed counterpurchase obligations by 24 suppliers as of April 1983. Of the $200 million in commitments assumed by the suppliers, about $144 million had been fulfilled by that date.

With hindsight and allowing for the urgency created by the economic situation in 1981, it could be argued that less severe guidelines for countertrade would have permitted counterpurchases of nontra-

Table 4
Status of Indonesian Counterpurchase Arrangements as of April 1983

Name of Supplier and Goods Supplied	Value of Counterpurchase (000 US$)	Goods Purchased	Value (000 US$)	Counterpurchase Balance (000 US$)
Kuok, Singapore (fertilizer)	2,384	Pollard	3,008	+623
Woodward & Dickerson, U.S. (fertilizer)	2,742	Crum rubber	1,857	−884
Amitrex, U.S. (fertilizer)	6,332	Rubber and coffee	6,379	+46
Philips, Netherlands (10 multicontrol systems)	4,920	Tin, cocoa liquor, toys, tea, cream latex	4,996	+75
Setia Sapta, W. Germany (generator set)	756	Plywood	814	+57
Fred Lekker, W. Germany (fertilizer)	8,378	Plywood	4,111	−4,226
Hart Tindo, Singapore (fertilizer)	18,500	Garments, rubber	5,758	−12,741
Mitsubishi, Japan (fertilizer)	23,193	Palm stearin, plywood, aluminum ingot, sawn timber, frozen prawn	16,850	−6,342

I.C.E.C., U.S. (fertilizer)	33,378	Rubber, coffee cacao, black pepper	38,302	+4,924
Nissho Iwai, Japan (plywood machinery, veneer)	6,461	Rattan mate, frozen prawn, fish oil, textile material, logs, aluminium, textiles,	1,510	−4,951
Kali Bergbau and Chemie Export Import, E. Germany (fertilizer)	7,310	Coal, nickel, garments, veneer, pepper	2,023	−5,287
San Giorgio, Italy (industrial equipment)	1,120	Rubber	579	−540
Danubiana, Rumania (fertilizer)	19,080	Rubber	9,202	−9,877
L. M. Ericson, Sweden (industrial equipment)	1,701	Black pepper, rubber, wood	1,026	−734
Hyosung, Korea (drum sheet)	9,598	Rubber, coal	904	−8,694
Transcontinental, U.S. (fertilizer)	5,100	Plywood	421	−4,679
Klockner H.D., W. Germany (calciner supply)	7,288	Tea, tin, rubber	4,005	−3,283

Table 4
Status of Indonesian Counterpurchase Arrangements as of April 1983 (*Continued*)

Name of Supplier and Goods Supplied	Value of Counterpurchase (000 US$)	Goods Purchased	Value (000 US$)	Counterpurchase Balance (000 US$)
Sydney Steel Co., Canada	9,758	Tea, rubber latex, tin	4,548	−5,210
Reed Rock Bit Company, Singapore (drill for Pertamina)	5,425	Black tea	2,985	−2,439
Uni Cane, Singapore	1,128	Rattan	100	−1,027
C. Itoh, Japan (coal mining, project under negotiation)	12,906	Sugar liquor, frozen prawn, jellyfish food, fresh prawn, veneer, copper, palm oil	6,623	−6,283
C. Itoh, Japan (sugar mill)	13,199	Palm oil, sugar liquor, frozen prawn, jelly fish, aluminium ingot, rubber wood, ethyl alcohol	5,478	−7,722

C. Itoh, Japan (refinery project)	N/A	Palm oil, logs, rubber, fresh prawn, veneer, frozen prawn, boiled crayfish, calalang fish, meranti wood	18,431
Nissho Iwai, Japan (refinery project)	N/A	Wood, animal bone, plywood, coffee, fish, textiles, frozen prawn, rubber, copper concentrate	4,450

ditional as well as traditional export goods, would have provided western exporters with alternatives to counterpurchase obligations tied to investments in joint marketing and other ventures benefiting the Indonesian economy, and would have created incentives for Indonesian exporters (e.g., export finance programs, advisory services, fiscal deferrals) to encourage them to investigate and get involved with countertrade arrangements.

chapter

6

Compensatory Arrangements as a Tool of Trade

A drill bit salesman once stated that his customers did not want drills; they wanted holes. But you don't get one without the other. The same is true of compensatory practices. Exporters are interested in the practices only to achieve their goals of profit. Yet, in addition to bottom-line motivations, the way in which the desired results are achieved is important, if long-term market presence is a goal and costly pitfalls are to be avoided. In this chapter we shall examine the motivations of trading parties to enter CAs, the use of such practices as marketing and financial tools, common problems associated with CAs, and the types of arrangements where CAs are most successful.

Motivations for Compensatory Trade

CA rationales span economic and political arguments and reflect the personal perceptions of benefits and liabilities of the parties involved. Generally, CAs are undertaken whenever one or more of the following conditions exist:

One or both trading parties lack sufficient foreign exchange reserves to pay for imports of goods and services intended for economic development, or they do not wish to use scarce foreign exchange reserves for trading.

The practice helps to sustain a country's export prices, which it intends to maintain at set levels in the face of declining demand.

A nation's exports are in low demand or they lack adequate distribution networks in foreign markets with which trade is desirable, and CAs help in creating markets for these exports.

Political or regional preference considerations justify bilateral trade linkages.

CAs offer importers a viable mode to gain access to foreign sources of raw materials, technology transfers, industrial manufacturing processes, and capital investment.

Whatever the conditions that foster compensatory practices, the trading parties will engage in such arrangements only if, in their assessment, the expected benefits outweigh the transactions' liabilities (the latter often being underestimated because of inexperience or inadequate foresight and preparation).

Probably, the major motivation for exporters to engage in CAs is the belief that CAs offer an option that could preserve market shares or increase trade levels in the face of credit constraints, foreign exchange restrictions, and import limitations. In addition to profit motives, some western exporters of capital equipment or aircraft justify their involvement with CAs on criteria ranging from preservation of production levels and employment, to amortization of development and other incurred costs. These manufacturers will take into account their integrated costs associated with the loss of the export opportunity when weighing whether to engage in individual CAs, and may choose to get involved in some transactions even when the profits derived may not be particularly attractive.

For western firms contemplating future expansion of their production capacity, compensation arrangements may also offer the opportunity to acquire a temporary supply source from the developing country until the western firm decides to undertake expansion of its own production. Furthermore, a long-term agreement may be reached whereby the sides could stagger their plant expansions sequentially. In this way they could provide each other with goods from their surplus capacities and could time the expansions to conform to world market needs, thus optimizing capital investment. Table 5 summarizes some major motivations that might influence a western exporter and a developing-country importer to engage in reciprocal trade under the auspices of a long-term CA contract which may include provisions for countertrade, coproduction, or equity investment.

Critics of CAs contend, and rightly so, that these practices increase the costs of trade and distort its patterns, and that they emphasize short-term or temporary needs over the orderly, long-term development of selective export positions. In the spirit of Adam Smith's eighteenth-century basic beliefs, they argue that unfettered, competitive markets are the most efficient allocators of resources. However, today's globally interdependent economic malaise and the narrowing of the communication gap and widening of the resource gap between the industrialized and the developing worlds, together with the explosive short-fused social challenges created by current unemployment levels, are fostering pressures which may not afford us the time to wait for self-induced market readjustments. Thus realities in the marketplace are overtaking approaches proven successful in the past and are motivating exporters and importers alike, albeit with reluctance, to explore CAs as a vehicle that can be responsive to pressing needs on both sides to sustain production and trade levels.

Compensatory Arrangements as Marketing and Financing Tools

Some exporters who agree to engage in CAs do so because it allows them to make sales which, because of the foreign exchange shortage of their customers, might otherwise be lost. Others accede to compensatory obligations imposed by their customers in order to gain an edge on the competition. In either case, the marketing drive is evident. On their part, importers enforcing compensatory commitments also use

Table 5
Motivations Resulting in Long-Term Compensatory Arrangements

Motivations		
Developing-Country Importer	**Western Exporter**	**Best-Suited Projects**
To obtain foreign technology know-how, management, marketing expertise and capital, and by virtue of the long-term relationship, to assure that such technology is kept current and responsive to world market demands To develop and promote joint research activities	To maximize return on past research and development investments, especially when technologies are becoming obsolescent and subject to constant improvements To increase the amount of control over the partner's marketing or production activities, so as to protect own investment	Projects requiring substantial fixed capital investment or advanced technology which is unavailable locally and which is considered vital for the importing country's economic development
To improve the country's trade position by import substitution, export stimulation and diversification To fulfill industrial and consumer needs which are growing at a rapid rate	To take advantage of local availability of unused factory capacity, raw materials, and stable and inexpensive labor force To assure a share in the local market growth and to acquire a competitive edge on other firms operating in the same geographic region	Projects for the manufacture of goods that fulfill domestic country market needs in the developing country
To gain access to the marketing networks of the foreign partner, develop collaboration in third markets, and acquire or improve marketing skills	To reduce transportation or production costs for exports To penetrate third markets through the developing country's regional or bilateral trade arrangements	Export-oriented projects that upgrade local goods or raw materials and provide the developing country with a positive foreign exchange balance

the leverage provided by their purchasing power in a buyer's-market environment, so as to develop export markets for their countries' products which may lack adequate marketing networks.

We have seen that Indonesia, as a sign of its seriousness to expand exports and in order to bind foreign suppliers to their counterpurchase commitments, has introduced a stiff 50 percent penalty clause in its government procurement contracts affecting nonfullfilment of compensatory obligations. Faced with protectionistic attitudes in the west against their industrial exports, the Soviet-bloc countries have also increased their penalty clause levels above the 10 to 15 percent asked in past years, in order to prevent western companies from building the penalty fee into their export prices and then opting to pay it. Indonesia and, in many cases, the Soviet-bloc countries also require that exports of counterdeliveries occur to specified destinations, so as not to interfere with these countries' own marketing arrangements abroad. Thus, these provisions are primarily designed to promote additional exports to foreign markets and to lend themselves best to indirect-compensation transactions where the goods to be marketed are in surplus or in low demand in export markets.

Other countries favor the use of CAs as a financing tool, especially for construction projects such as industrial plants. Buyback arrangements requiring annual counterdeliveries of plant output in the range of 20 to 30 percent would recover for the importer the entire cost of the foreign-supplied plant in a few years. In the early 1970s, the Soviet Union undertook an ambitious industrialization program involving the establishment of considerable chemical production capacity to be paid for through exports of plant output (see examples in Appendix C). As a result, Soviet methanol, ammonia, and other chemicals are now being marketed in several western countries.

The People's Republic of China has also been looking at CAs as a vehicle to finance its industrial base. Following internal debates, China decided in mid-1978 to actively encourage direct-compensation transactions through duty rebates benefiting imports of western machinery, materials, know-how, and technologies acquired by existing plants, and to be repaid with exports derived from processing finished goods or components in these refurbished plants. It was intended that such trade would contribute to the modernization of about 350,000 obsolescent, small and medium-sized Chinese industrial enterprises serving regional needs. Indirect compensation, whereby the western exporter receives goods which are not related to his export, was not to be facilitated or favored by national enterprises.

The nature of most indirect-compensation transactions is to promote marketing of the importer's goods. Such transactions often involve surplus goods difficult to market at the prices at which they are being offered by the importing country. On the other hand, direct-compensation transactions, especially those involving new plant capacity, generally serve to fulfill financing requirements, and the resulting outputs are in grand part dedicated to domestic consumption needs. The latter arrangements offer exporters more latitude for generating creative options on how to fulfill compensatory obligations. Favorable financing terms or other arrangements (e.g., use of the importer's construction crews in projects undertaken by the western constructor in foreign countries) may be negotiated in the contract so as to decrease the proposed buyback commitment. In addition, the plant output could benefit from comparative advantages which may be reflected in the cost of the goods offered as compensation.

Special Problems of Compensatory Arrangements

When problems occur in a compensatory transaction, especially when dealing with developing-country importers, they can usually be traced to two sources: differences in the parties' commercial objectives and different methods of doing business. Gaining an early understanding of these potential problem areas allows for preventive action on the part of the exporter and helps him in introducing appropriate adjustments to export prices which account for incurred costs.

Differences in objectives mostly arise in the trade with developing countries. After allowing for the trading parties' obvious interest in gaining footholds in each other's markets without compromising established positions in their own, differences in objectives may result from:

The developing-country importer's limited technical needs related to his country's level of industrial development and his domestic market size

The western exporter's need to promote and market his own specialized product or technology, even when other competing products or technologies could be more cost-effective or appropriate to the importer's limited needs

The importer's need to provide adequate incentives which would attract long-term investment of foreign resources and thus assure him of partaking in technology advances and provide him with access to the foreign party's marketing network

The western exporter's need to derive quick returns on sales or investments, so as to hedge against market risks and to justify the company's business performance to his stockholders on an annual basis

The importer's need to impose compensatory obligations on the western exporter

The western exporter's desire to avoid, whenever possible, such obligations

Other factors contributing to differences in commercial objectives may relate to dissimilar concepts of profit in the trading parties' economic systems. For example, in communist economies, profit is viewed as mainly a return on sales or capital investment, rather than a blend which includes returns on such committed resources as management, technical services, and marketing. Also contributing to misunderstandings is the poor grasp by some developing countries of the American marketing system which (a) relies on extensive and costly research, market tests, and advertising in introducing a new product to the U.S. market, (b) provides protective safeguards for the consumer through government regulations, through assignment of responsibility for product liability, and involves extensive after-sale services, and (c) consists of a multitier distribution system which includes the importer, the wholesaler, the distributor, and finally the retailer. While differences in views on the above issues can affect the likelihood of contracting an agreement, it is mainly the differing ways of doing business, following the contract signing, that have the potential to affect the costs of CAs assumed by a western company. Such problems could result from:

Shortcomings with the counterdelivered products resulting from design models that do not conform to western style and taste; costs incurred by the western importer prior to marketing because of the need to repackage or refurbish the products; poor quality-control standards used in the manufacture of the products; unavailability of spares and components; noncompetitive pricing and unreliable delivery schedules; and any inability to provide after-sale services to customers.

Differences in the methods of doing business, which include long reaction times to western requests for information and the slow pace in reaching decisions, as most developing-country officials or exporters are not risk takers but perform under government guidelines.

Bureaucratic impediments in developing countries, which include requirements for import permits and other reviews; limitations on the spectrum of goods made available as counterdeliveries; and limitations on linking to western exports counterpurchases from more than one manufacturer in the developing country. These limitations may be imposed by government policies or may result from the difficulty of receiving the necessary authorizations from the two or more ministries involved.

Any evaluation of results of the western company's involvement in compensatory transactions should weigh the costs and problems of such operations against benefits resulting from related sales of the firm's goods, know-how, services, technology, and spares. It also should note indirect benefits, such as the familiarization of the export market with the company goods, forestalling of competition of other firms operating in the same market, spin-off trade opportunities in third countries where the counterdeliveries are marketed, and the use of existing production overcapacity abroad. In a particular instance, a U.S. company was able to postpone its capital investments for a new chemical plant because of exclusive marketing rights to the chemical obtained against the sale of technology to an eastern European country.

Products Available for Compensatory Trade

The volume of direct-compensation transactions (involving counterdeliveries derived from the western export) which is related to the erection of new plant facilities in developing countries is leveling off because of current constraints in credit and markets. Instead, the trend is to finance expansions or modernizations of existing production facilities through the sale of products processed in these facilities. For example, direct-compensation trade on a limited scale entailing the processing and assembly of light industry manufactures such as textiles, garments, leather goods, and appliances is on the increase in the People's Republic of China's areas bordering Hong Kong and Macao as well as in other provinces and municipalities with access to ports, overland shipping facilities, and strong traditional ties to overseas Chinese communities.

Indirect-compensation deliveries available as counterpurchases vary for each country according to several factors. These include the type and volume of goods produced by the country each year (some countries prefer to offer nontraditional export products); the demand for the goods in export markets (goods salable for hard currency may not be made available for counterpurchase); and the period of the year (the last quarter of the calendar year may be the best time to buy, if the developing-country exporter is trying to fulfill his export targets). Governments may also influence the type of exports available for counterdelivery. Some governments allow counterpurchases from the entire spectrum of goods available in the country, as in New Zealand; others seek to restrict counterdeliveries to the industrial sector which imported the foreign goods, as in most communist countries, or to the importing region, as in Yugoslavia's republics; still other governments specify the goods they will allow as counterpurchases, as in Ecuador which exempts petroleum and shrimp counterpurchases in private transactions.

In regard to counterpurchases originating in eastern European countries and the Soviet Union, exporting enterprises are instructed on the annual export and counterpurchase quotas assigned to them. These quotas, coordinated by the Ministry of Foreign Trade, are derived from a listing of goods that are produced for export or are expected to exceed domestic needs. The quotas take into account (according to certain established formulas) the projected production and availability of goods produced locally, their allocation by previous commitments, their marketability on export markets, the country's projected payment and trade balance for the year, and the requirements for certain industrial sectors to export production not absorbed by the domestic market.

Products such as raw materials or certain commodities that can be sold without difficulty in hard-currency markets may be made available for counterpurchase in Soviet-bloc countries only when necessary to ensure high-priority western imports, and they are quickly used up. These products will appear on lists of goods offered for export and/or counterpurchase to western exporters even when such goods may no longer be available. Delivery of counterpurchase goods chosen from such lists is subordinated to any export bids the communist exporting enterprise may receive for these goods prior to the commitment deadline to the western party. Also, manufacturing scheduled to fulfill counterpurchase commitments has a low priority in the communist countries' production planning. Thus delivery delays of counterpurchased goods are common, and these products may be of poor quality, may lack spares and after-sale service, and may have inadequate packaging.

Authorization to link counterpurchases from more than one exporting enterprise may involve two or more ministries, thus complicating the transaction. Whenever excess production which is not slated for export becomes available because of lack of coordinated planning (e.g., feedstock chemicals destined for a plant whose completion runs beyond schedule), these goods may also be offered for counterpurchasing. The same is true of any surplus goods obtained as a result of the communist country's bilateral clearing agreements with developing countries (e.g., dates from Iraq imported into Bulgaria, cotton from Pakistan imported into Romania).

Although the use of countertrade is expected to increase during coming years as an integral part of many developing countries' economic planning, these countries' planners recognize that certain countertrade transactions are not in the best interest of the development of trade with the industrialized countries. Related factors that may limit expansion of the practices are:

The spotty availability of sufficient volumes of counterdeliveries for the many countertrade transactions proposed

The substandard quality and lack of after-sales service for many of the manufactures offered as counterpurchases

The opposition of most western firms to countertrade, which stems from their inability to handle counterpurchase arrangements and which limits the number of western companies doing business in markets enforcing the practice

The concern of some developing-country exporters that a western firm may dump the acquired counterpurchases in their own export markets

Where Compensatory Trade Is More Successful

Success in compensatory trade often acquires for an exporter different meanings from those associated with traditional sales. While traditional sales success may be measured only by the profits generated through sales, in compensatory trade it also includes spin-off benefits, e.g., the ability of an exporter to retain foreign market shares, circumvent foreign currency restrictions, support operations of his subsidiaries abroad, secure minimum cash flow requirements for his operations, and maintain his domestic production lines in operation without loss of employment. From this perspective, the additional costs related to CAs could be looked upon as necessary expenditures of doing business in markets where the western exporter needs to retain a presence, and should be regarded as an integral part of marketing costs along with advertising and other promotional expenses.

Judging from the number of contracted compensatory projects which have been reported, the most successful type of CA involves direct-compensation transactions. These span from erection of new production capacity and extraction and processing of mineral resources, to processing of materials or assembly of finished goods making use of existing plant capacity. The latter type of CA is becoming more common today, given the worldwide slowdown on construction of new plant capacity. It offers western firms the advantage of securing competitively priced goods with marginal investment of capital, training, and equipment. It has, on the other hand, the disadvantage of being restricted—at least in the developing countries—to transactions in the light industry sector, wherein much of the existing production capacity of these countries lies.

An example of a CA involving processing of materials is the 1979 agreement between the American firm AMF and the Shanghai Number 3 Rubber Products Factory. Under the 10-year agreement, AMF has lent manufacturing equipment and is providing materials to the factory in return for production of 340,000 rubber sports balls per year. The contract provides that after the 10-year loan of the equipment, the factory has the option to purchase it at a price to be negotiated. Because the equipment supplied by AMF to the factory is being paid for through counterdeliveries of goods rather than through currencies, the transaction qualifies as a CA.

Of the counterdelivered goods, those easier to dispose of are goods that can be absorbed by the western exporter within its own company and within those of his clients and subcontractors, or that can be marketed and serviced through the western exporter's distribution network. These counterdeliveries may consist of commodities or components and finished goods manufactured to the western firm's specification. Many countries prefer that their counterdeliveries be indeed absorbed within the western supplier's organization or, at least, within his country of origin, so as not to interfere or compete with the country's own foreign exports.

At the other extreme, the most difficult CAs to conclude are those involving western exporters with narrow fields of specialization and single-type products. For instance, a manufacturer of machinery or equipment slated to upgrade production of an importer's plant may face a most difficult task in disposing of the modernized plant's output received in countertrade, given his narrow marketing specialization and the likely marginal quality or obsolescent design of many such plants' products, especially those which service domestic needs in developing countries. The western exporter may also have difficulty in finding a broker willing to market the finished goods unless these are heavily discounted or the size of the transaction provides the broker with adequate profit margins.

Figure 6.1 illustrates a rule-of-thumb evaluation of the degree of expected difficulty in disposing of counterdeliveries derived from five different types of countertrade transactions. Also suggested in the figure are the likely intermediaries for handling the counterdeliveries.

In addition to marketing considerations concerning the goods ob-

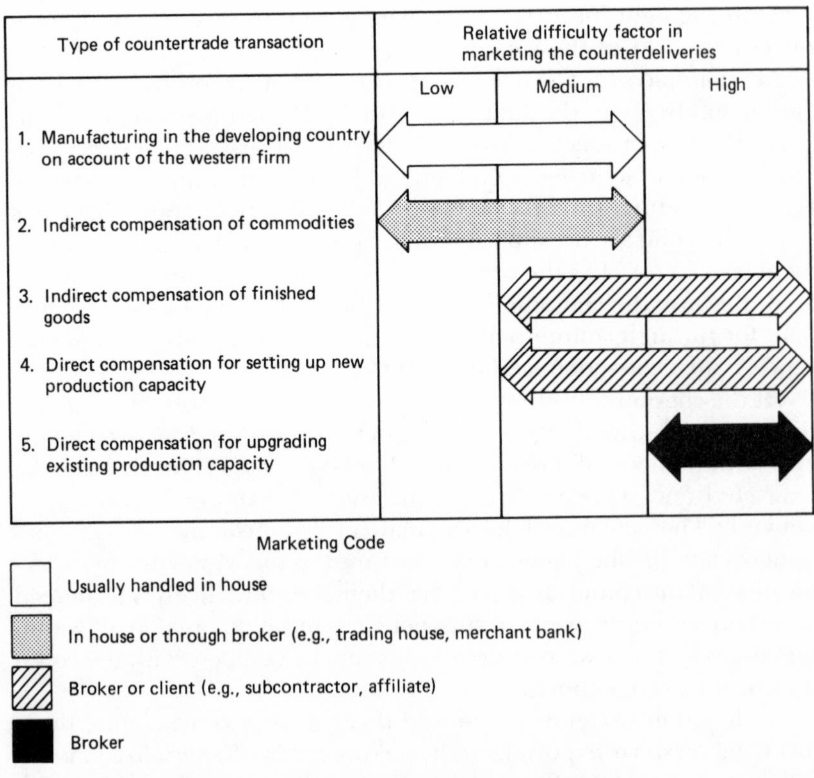

Figure 6.1. Expected difficulty factor in marketing countertrade goods.

tained as countertrade, successful completion of any CA depends on several qualitative factors which include:

The degree of flexibility and acquaintance with compensatory practices by both trading parties

The understanding of the parties' reciprocal limitations in making or requiring concessions, and the matching of their commercial objectives

The transaction's priority for the importer as reflected in the allocation of at least some foreign exchange for the imports

The uniqueness of the exporter's equipment and technology, as well as the attractiveness of his commercial terms

The risk assessment of the CA under evaluation (discussed also in Chapter 8) in relation to the benefits derived by the exporter

The existence of a coordinating bureaucratic structure within the importing country which can facilitate linkage of counterdeliveries within and across industrial sectors

The existence of government-sponsored incentives in the importing country which benefit CAs (e.g., import and export duty and fiscal rebates for the country's domestic importers)

The factors described in this section, whose evaluation for most CAs involves advance preparation and homework on the part of the western exporter, will contribute to his propensity, or lack thereof, to engage in CAs.

chapter

7

Planning and Strategies

The atmosphere of economic and political uncertainty which is affecting an increasing number of nations, in particular those of the third world, requires the adoption of revised planning concepts and marketing programs on the part of western exporters.

Marketing strategies in the 1980s will have to strike an acceptable compromise between a western company's desire for quick results, involving limited risk exposure in uncertain export markets, and a developing nation's desire to secure long-term access to western capital, know-how, technology, and markets through joint cooperation arrangements such as CAs. Conditions in many export markets in the 1980s may require concentrating the company's resources and efforts on selective markets instead of striking out at tactical targets of opportunity or pursuing export initiatives on a worldwide scale. Marketing will require:

Long-term strategic planning for market development, which involves current understanding of the evolving political, social, and regional influences as well as of risk factors in the targeted export markets, rather than market planning based only on demographic factors and annual economic indicators

Development of programs and strategies that will include options providing for sourcing of materials and labor in markets targeted for a company's exports, rather than including only exports of western finished goods and turnkey projects

Acceptance of CAs as one of the available tools—along with others such as pricing and investment—for preserving or enhancing the exporter's market share

Above all, marketing will require the development of a creative and capable middle-management staff with the ability to suggest and implement flexible approaches to the particular conditions that may face the company in individual export markets.

The Management

Managers of too many western companies have grown up in an environment that stresses caution over creative and opportunistic decision making. Formed in the business climate of the past decades—when extension of liberal credit and sustained global economic growth hedged their risks—and schooled in conventionally established business management methods, these managers' objectives have stressed short-term profit growth and have been mainly concerned with limiting downside risk, rather than with gaining upside rewards through entrepreneurship.

Today the more farseeing companies are redirecting their efforts—albeit under pressure from the rapidly changing market environment—to develop improved strategies at the business unit level, that of the product line or related product lines. They are also expanding the role of the company's middle management from that of implementer of marketing goals formulated by higher executive levels, to that of entrepreneur expected to devise opportunistic and creative approaches to the problems encountered in their areas of individual responsibility. Such tactics, shaped by the company's long-range goals and incorporated into a plan of action, are expected to provide the necessary guidance for the company's units which will permit them to fulfill their assigned roles within the corporate plan.

In addition to identifying markets, customers, competitors, government regulations, and threats to their business, effective middle-management staff action will have to include suggestions on best-suited matchings between product mixes and changing market needs, inputs concerning vulnerabilities and risks, and methods to achieve the company's prescribed goals in individual markets. In other words, the success of a company's operations in the competitive trade environment of the 1980s will depend on adding to the responsibilities of middle-management personnel who have been most burdened in the past with day-to-day operating problems and have not dedicated much time to the assessment of emerging trends in export markets or to the formulation of hedging operations. Success will also depend on harnessing personnel who can divorce themselves from strategies which have been successful in the past and adopt creative, flexible, and entrepreneurial approaches which lend themselves to the opportunities and problems of the present.

At corporate levels, management may have to exchange the tranquility of paced, albeit slow, growth for the challenge of opportunistic business development. Rather than considering planning as solely a numbers game or a way to manage assets, corporate executives will have to be able to develop flexible strategies which will cope with emerging problems and opportunities in markets on a worldwide basis. Such strategies may involve diversification of the company's resources and markets, may tackle productivity problems or materials shortages through subcontracting or sourcing abroad, when necessary, and may integrate the activities of all of the company's business units for the fulfillment of occasional tasks such as those related to CA requirements.

An essential ingredient of corporate management in the 1980s will be the creation of a climate that encourages new ideas, accepts change, has patience with long-term results, and stimulates the free flow of information, both of the concrete and practical type generated from the bottom up and of the conceptual and strategic type generated from the top down. Chief executives, nurtured on years of past successful operating experience, will also have to shift emphasis from project-oriented thinking and from accounting planning to strategic thinking. This evolution and familiarization with new business practices such as CAs will likely require several years of assimilation for a majority of today's standing corporate executives.

Corporate boards may also have to find palatable strategies that provide for unpopular short-term setbacks, in order to secure long-range market positions whose results extend beyond the typical 7- to 8-year board tenures. They will have to devise incentive programs designed to compensate line managers for long-term rather than annual results, and will have to formulate policies which will allocate corporate resources to business units according to the degree of risk and reward involved. Above all, they will have to encourage staffing criteria which will secure or breed appropriate mixes of entrepreneurs and long-range planners among their personnel so as to anticipate and successfully react to threats as well as opportunities in the market.

Planning for Compensatory Trade

CAs represent only one of the options available to the exporter for market entry or preservation of market shares, along with such other alternatives as licensing, leasing, and investment. The use of CAs may be specified in the marketing plan aimed at a target market or project, or it may be considered a contingent alternative of the general marketing strategy of the company. The plan itself becomes a living (i.e., adaptable) document whose worth depends on how well it embodies the company's corporate values, on the quality and flow of information it draws on, and on the degree of flexibility for revision it provides.

The corporate values of the company refer to its prevailing policies on exporting and general criteria for involvement in foreign markets, its availability and allocation of resources to export, and the characteristics of its products and technologies. The quality and flow of information refers to top-down flow of corporate and strategic thinking, bottom-up flow of market information sourced by the firm's business units, and any necessary information acquired from other sources such as government agencies, banks, insurance companies, specialized brokers, and consultants. In today's changing trade climate of limited opportunities and rising risks, the importance of securing access to diversified sources of current intelligence and of acquiring the ability to assess the information within the context of a marketing plan cannot be overemphasized.

Information flow, corporate value, and resources set the framework for development of the firm's marketing goals within the overall corporate strategic plan. Through market assessment, evaluation of alternatives, and creation of strategic initiatives, the plan extends the company's current methods of operation and seeks to improve the company's competitiveness by attempting to predict and create the future. The steps in developing a marketing strategy are:

The selection of a target market
The identification of market objectives

The choice of market-entry modes

The monitoring of market performance and the adjustments to achieve desired results

The marketing plan for each product defines a course of action over a prescribed period of time, which may vary from one to several years, and sets desired objectives in a target export market. Figure 7.1 illustrates these steps in more detail. In mapping strategies within marketing plans, the planners should also:

Take into consideration the inclination, or lack thereof, of the company's leadership to support over the long run unorthodox marketing approaches such as CAs.

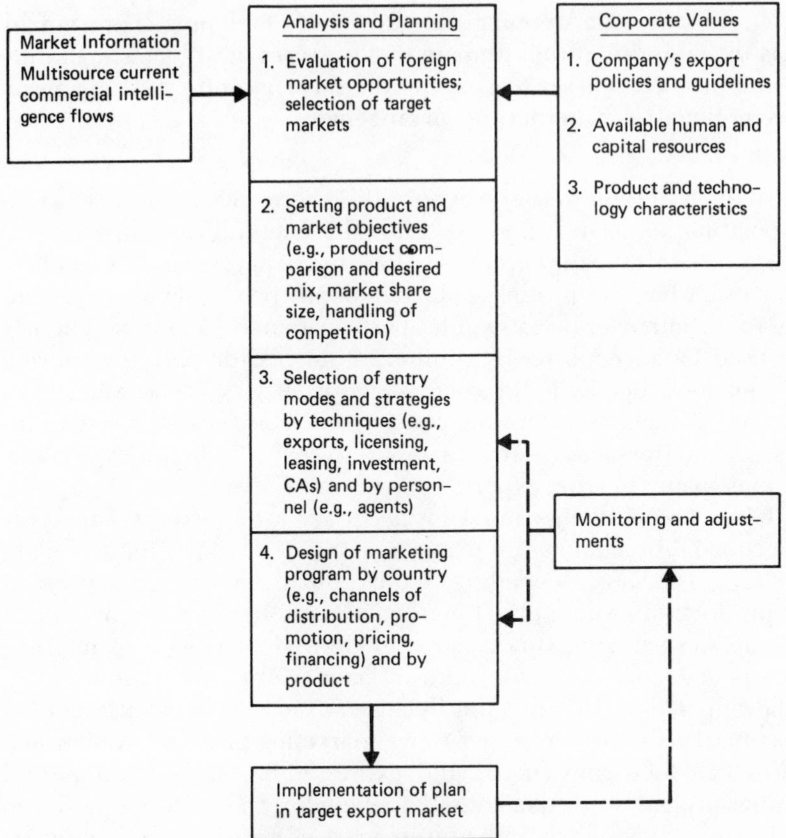

Figure 7.1. International marketing strategy evolution.

- Identify sources of outside assistance for CAs—e.g., consultants, banks, trading houses, other specialized brokers, company clients and subcontractors receptive to sharing compensatory obligations—and suggest in-house organizational and logistical steps designed to facilitate handling of CAs.
- Establish to what degree CAs should be treated as marketing tools to be used for the enhancement of export sales—and thus be subsidized, if necessary, as would be promotional advertising—or as profitable sources of supplies.
- Set market priorities based not only on the market's economic potential, size, and political stability, but also on such considerations as the sophistication of the country's banking and industrial infrastructure as well as the competence and performance track record of its bureaucratic structure; the country's policies and enacted legislation concerning the facilitation of trade and foreign investment; the possibilities it offers to serve as a stepping stone to other developing-country markets through use of the company's subsidiaries or affiliates operating in the primary market (e.g., using the former country's credit facilities, regional or bilateral trade arrangement).

In analyzing the western exporter's investment of resources in an export market against derived returns, it is useful to compare these quantities with the importer's own investment and returns. Identification and, whenever possible, valuation of any potential benefits accruing to the importer because of his participation in the transaction may be used by an exporter as counterarguments for parrying, during negotiations, demands for concessions or, at least, as arguments to extract, in turn, reciprocating concessions.Table 6 lists a range of invested resources and returns that may accrue to both parties in transactions spanning from exports to direct investment.

If resource limitations make it necessary for an exporter to apply selection criteria among his export markets, the criteria for action are not always obvious. Depending on the compatibility of a given product or product mix with a target market, and on the resource investment by the western company relative to derived benefits, the matrices shown in Figure 7.2 could be used as rule-of-thumb indicators for follow-up action. In evaluating relative attractiveness of different export markets as part of a long-range marketing program, similar matrices could be constructed and expressed in terms of numerical ratings instead of the qualitative low, medium, and high ranges shown in Figure 7.2. For a particular target market, matrices could be super-

Table 6
Potential Resource Commitments and Derived Benefits of Trading Parties Involved in Long-Term Arrangements

Party	Resource Investments	Derived Benefits
Developing-country importer	• Labor • Existing production capacity • Materials • Fiscal and/or other incentives • Capital	• Sustained production • Utilization of labor force • Access to technology and know-how • Exposure to future technical innovations • Improved production standards • Upgrading of labor skills • Upgrading of marketing skills • Expansion of markets (domestic or foreign) • Access to the foreign partner's resources with limited risk exposure • Spin-off benefits to other domestic industries • Impetus for R&D • Increase in tax base
Western exporter	• Technical personnel • Capital • Equipment • Countertrade-related expenditures • Marketing skills/network • Technology and know-how • Risks associated with dependence on new supply source; creation of potential competitor; postponement of increasing own production capacity	• Export sales • Access to developing-country market(s) • Access to alternative source of supply • Reduction of transportation costs • Reduction of production costs • Increase in production capacity • Utilization of low-cost labor force

imposed evaluating such factors as political risk, market size, economic growth, regulatory policies, and practices affecting trade. The end result of such an exercise is to develop marketing programs providing for selective allocation of company resources in preferred target markets.

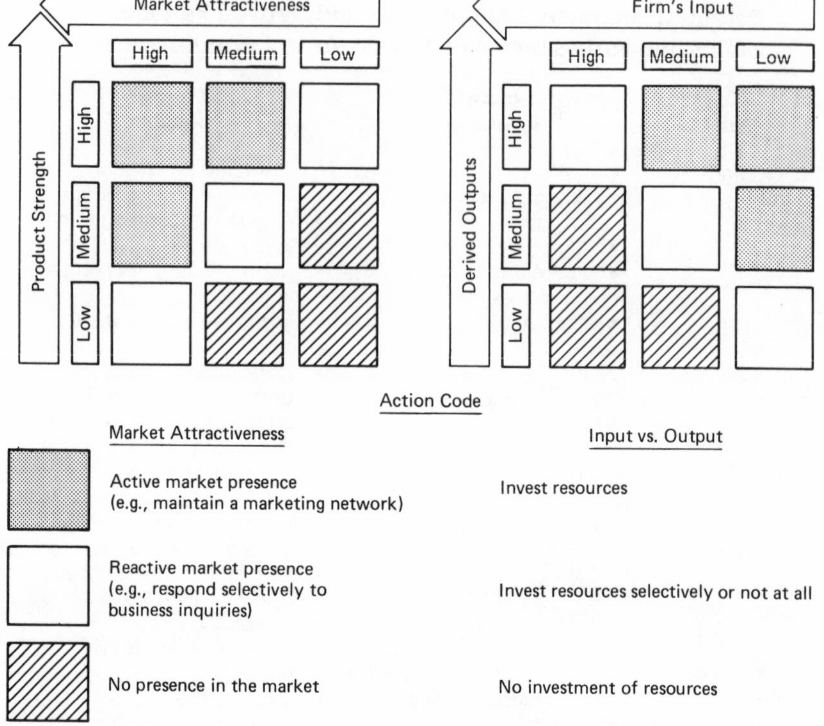

Figure 7.2. Market vs. product and resource input vs. desired output indicator matrices.

Companies which expect to encounter, or are already confronted with, compensatory demands in their export markets face alternative options: avoiding these markets altogether; negotiating price discounts and other concessions in lieu of assuming compensatory obligations; or devising steps that would permit them to accede to the demands and handle the obligations profitably. Preventive planning based on assessment of market trends and timely information (e.g., the priority assigned to the export by the importer, the nature of the import restrictions and their applicability to the transaction under consideration) can benefit the exporter by identifying at an early stage the potential problems in his markets and the related costs of operation. It may also provide the exporter with the necessary lead time to influence in his favor an importer's compensatory policies or, alternatively, time to adjust the terms of the export offer so as to satisfy any limitations under which the importer is obliged to operate. Figure 7.3

is a decision tree diagram illustrating the options available to exporters who are confronted by compensatory pressures in their export markets.

Negotiation Strategies

The first line of defense against compensatory impositions is at the negotiation table. Exporters should try to determine from the onset of negotiations whether the transaction under discussion will involve

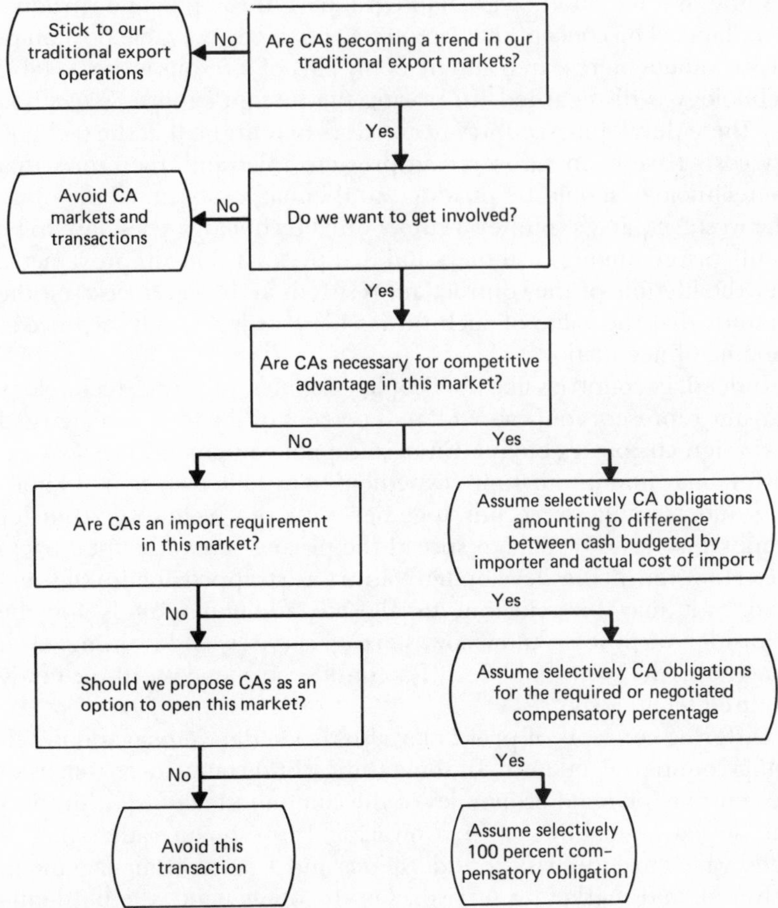

Figure 7.3. Compensatory-arrangement decision tree.

compensatory obligations and how much these requirements are likely to cost. This might be difficult if the importer chooses to wait until late in the negotiations before raising the issue of compensation. Thus, it is important to invest time in advance preparation aimed at identifying the applicable strategies, the needs, and the policies of the importer (if these are not public knowledge) as well as to invest time in devising varied fallback options or counterproposals to be advanced as substitutes for compensatory obligations.

An exporter's advance preparation should include familiarization with the customer's traditional viewpoints on purchasing, so as to be able to convey more effectively the western viewpoint. For instance, some developing countries view technology transfer as an asset only in so far as it is embodied as an integral part of equipment or production plants. The concept that western firms spend a sizable portion of sales revenues on research and that only part of it results in marketable technology is disregarded. In pricing the foreign exporter's technology, these developing-country negotiators may argue that the technology costs have been recovered in previous sales and, therefore, that the technology should be provided to them at a substantial discount. The western party's counterargument that technology sales have to be evenly priced among customers and that prices include improvements over the lifetime of the contract are resisted, in the latter case, on the grounds that the value of such future benefits is difficult to prove at the time of negotiations.

Indeed, in countries like the People's Republic of China, technology transfer represents only about 2 to 3 percent of the total cost charged to foreign customers buying Chinese capital equipment. Western exporters may find it sometimes expedient to include transfers of know-how and training programs together with the technology-transfer proposal, so as to be able to spread the pricing across the total package. However, if the developing country is strapped for foreign exchange, it may be reluctant to allocate additional funds for the acquisition of process know-how, start-up services, and training, even though this decision could delay for considerable time use of the newly acquired technology.

Differing concepts of profit may also divide the western and developing-country negotiators. In some third world countries as well as in the centrally planned economies of the communist countries, profit is still viewed as mainly a return on capital investment rather than a blend which includes risk considerations and a range of management, technical, and marketing services. On the other hand, the hard-currency prices of the developing country's counterdeliveries are likely to be set just below estimated world-market price levels. Such inflated prices exceed real social, material, and labor costs and are usually prescribed by the developing country's government agencies.

Western exporters should also become aware of any limitations under which the other side at the negotiation table operates. In the communist countries and some other countries with controlling bureaucratic structures, such limitations are well established. In negotiating, these importers are not risk takers or entrepreneurs, but perform under imposed guidelines. Their dominant motivation is fear of assuming responsibility rather than the desire to see the transaction implemented, and they may fear their peers' opinions about their competence as negotiators. Thus, their strict adherence to paperwork, specs, and regulations is intended to avoid blame for any unforeseen shortcomings. This attitude could protract negotiations and may involve abiding by detailed product certifications to which the western exporter is unaccustomed and which increase his export costs. An experienced western negotiator will take into consideration his counterpart's attitudes and enforced predicament. The exporter will agree and guarantee in writing to "make up any deficiencies from contracted terms of sale," supplanting the necessity to conform with all of the importer's technicalities and paperwork, easing his task in securing approval from superiors, and shielding him from direct responsibility.

If the exporter is prepared to accept a CA, he will have to quote a price that makes allowance for any costs he expects to incur, such as those involving the marketing of any counterdeliveries he receives in payment. If, on the other hand, he is not willing to assume any compensatory obligations, he should so advise the importer at the beginning of negotiations. It is important to realize from the onset that the obligation of most developing-country importers is to extract the highest possible level of compensatory concessions, according to directives passed down by their government agencies. Although normal negotiating and testing gambits dictate that initial compensatory demands be high, the final requirement agreed upon in the contract may be much lower and will depend on official approval. High-priority imports necessary to the fulfillment of national economic development or which generate hard-currency exports may require little or no compensatory obligations, while imports of capital equipment and industrial plants for which no foreign exchange has been allocated by the government, as well as imports of nonessential goods such as consumer and luxury articles, may require 100 percent CAs in some developing countries. In any case, it is good negotiating strategy to quote, whenever possible, final prices for exports only after the terms, conditions, and the product range of countertrade goods offered are identified.

If an exporter faced with countertrade demands has not already consulted with trading houses or other experts and has not already secured a commitment for the disposal of the counterdeliveries, his price quotation will have to reflect a best-estimate guess concerning all marketing expenses he is likely to incur, inclusive of transportation costs. For example, the shipment of counterdeliveries to developing countries which could be targeted as potential markets for these goods may involve high costs if the destinations are not adequately serviced by transportation networks; or the deliveries may not provide the customers with the long-term source of supply they may desire.

Soviet-bloc negotiators in particular have been known to wait until the last minute before signing a contract to spring countertrade demands on western exporters. This known tactic has established the trend among western exporters to bury in their prices a conservatively estimated safety margin, thus transferring back to the importers the costs associated with the disposal of the countertraded goods.

An exporter confronted at the last minute with a request for CAs may face difficult decisions. The exporter may not want to offer a rebate in his quoted price instead of accepting the countertrade imposition, in order to maintain the credibility of his company's offer. He may want to find out during the course of the negotiations whether the importer will be satisfied with the payment of the prescribed penalty fee for nonfulfillment of the compensatory obligations, or whether such action would jeopardize future relations with the importer. Indonesia's official regulations specifying a stiff 50 percent penalty fee assessed on the unfulfilled portion of an exporter's counterpurchase obligations are intended to discourage payment of the fee in lieu of undertaking the marketing of Indonesian goods.

Exporters who choose to engage in CAs may consider a range of options in developing their negotiation strategies. For example, they could consider any one, or any combination, of the options listed below:

Negotiate lower compensatory terms in return for one or more concessions, for example:

- Price discounts
- Extension of repayment terms
- Extension of performance guarantees
- Expansion of training programs for the customer's personnel

- Increase in other export-related support services
- Guaranteed fixed prices over a specified period for all or part of the spares to be supplied under the terms of the contract
- Transfer of part or all of the compensatory obligations against a subsidy to a third party

Accept partial payment in local currencies, even when these are nonconvertible or cannot be transferred abroad, as long as the following are contractually stipulated and officially permitted:

- The currencies are transferable to third parties within the importer's country—for example, to defray costs of foreign subsidiaries residing there.
- The currencies can be used to defray the exporter's own costs in the importer's country, such as for lodgings, insurance, travel, conventions, or vacations for the exporting firm's personnel
- The currencies can be reinvested in the importer's country.

Accept partial payment in services made available by the customer's country domestically or abroad, such as those of construction and engineering crews to be used by the exporter in third countries.

Purchase, for a subsidy, the right to export to the customer's country under the import license or the contractual rights of some other company.

Assist in identifying business opportunities or create sales for the customer in foreign markets, with proceeds to be credited directly against the exporter's sales or remitted to a trust fund in a western country which has been set up to finance such sales.

Subcontract, license, or invest in other projects in the customer's country as part of the CAs.

Negotiate lower compensation commitments in return for guarantees to the customer to cooperate with him in marketing in third markets.

The option of reinvestment for any partial payments received in nonconvertible currencies will hinge on the developing countries' policies affecting foreign ownership of domestic assets such as real estate, stock, and equity. For example, some major U.S. banks operating in Brazil, being deterred from repatriating profits by stiff taxes on transfers, are reinvesting their cruzeiro profits in real estate as a hedge against inflation and taxation. Other multinational companies, such as the Italian firm Pirelli, are choosing to lend locally profits earned in Brazil rather than sending them home. To help meet foreign exchange scarcity and to encourage investment, the government of the Philippines recently issued guidelines to allow some domestic firms to convert their import costs into foreign-owned equity. Mexico is also modifying restrictive investment laws to welcome majority-owned foreign investments in specified industrial sectors with emphasis on export generation, import substitution, and labor-intensive investments.

When assuming counterpurchase commitments, exporters should be aware that many of the products offered as counterdeliveries may be unavailable because of prior commitments or limited production. Exporters should first select goods that can be absorbed within their own company or those of their clients or subcontractors. Such procedure is preferred by the country where the counterdeliveries are sourced, because the goods do not end up on foreign markets in potential competition with that country's own exports and because the price charged for the western exports will not include the passed-through costs associated with the disposal of the counterdeliveries.

Some western companies have found it advantageous to engage in anticipatory purchases in order to create goodwill and eventual credits for future exports devoid of countertrade obligations. If the anticipatory purchases involve large dollar values or long-term contracts, the western purchaser might be able to exert enough leverage on the supplier to secure the right to offset a portion of his purchases' value with future sales. In the case of long-term contracts, this portion will usually represent only incremental purchases by the western party above established trade levels (additionality requirement). As previously stated, this credit acquired by the purchaser is known as reverse countertrade or junktim, and when made transferable to third parties, it can be assigned against payment of a fee or subsidy to the third party.

chapter

8

Risks and Their Prevention in Compensatory Trade

Foreign risk assessment is rapidly becoming a permanent part of corporate management, as political events around the globe are forcing exporters to focus on the risks inherent in overseas operations. As a result, independent risk-assessment consulting services have multiplied and several major multinational manufacturing firms have developed in-house risk-analysis units, following the lead of banks and oil companies. While numerical risk indices and ratings—reflecting political stability of a country—have been widely used in the past, the trend of present risk analysis is directed toward studying and forecasting discriminatory attitudes by governments which would affect trade and investment, as unexpected shifts in official regulatory policies are raising greater concerns than the danger of expropriations.

In this vein, risks associated with CAs are scarcely understood. Current coverage of CAs is spotty among insurance companies and is an extension of existing risk policies (e.g., product liability, contract repudiation, and business interruption such as due to delays in contracted deliveries). Indeed, insurance companies often prefer to insure a transaction on deferred payment terms rather than to guarantee countertrade performance. In addition to administrative costs (say, about 20 percent of premium dollar), insurance firms tend to keep analysis cost for the individual transactions they insure down to a minimum and rely on the creditworthiness and reputation of the exporter to assess the viability of the transaction. This attitude limits, for the most part, coverage to large exporters who have established track records for competence in international trade and who are able to afford the premiums charged. On the other hand, it forgoes a realistic understanding of the risks the insurance company actually assumes. Today, project risk liability—which should be normally shouldered partially by government organizations of developing countries—is shifting back to the western exporter, his bank, and his insurance company because of the deterioration of the creditworthiness of many foreign countries. Because insurance companies have not yet brought in line their premium charges with their real exposure to risk, the potential exists of further coverage shrinkages for exporters, especially the smaller firms, in case of major future defaults.

Possible hedges against CA risk assumed by an exporter are: (1) a viable construed and priced commercial transaction, (2) a written contract which deals with identified exposures that the exporter has to assume, and (3) an insurance policy which covers insurable risk. The first two items clearly depend on the individual ability of the exporter to identify and assess the CA's risk, while the last one depends on his willingness to assume the insurance premium costs.

Risk Assessment of Compensatory Transactions

Major risk categories for an exporter, whether or not his transaction is a CA, can be summarized as follows:

Political risks resulting from adverse actions by recognized governments, such as:

- Seizure of assets (e.g., expropriation, unfair calling of financial guarantees)
- Interference with contractual performance (e.g., contract repudiation or termination without rightful cause, interference by laws and regulations enacted after the contract has been signed and which affect its performance)
- Import or export license cancellation
- Currency inconvertibility
- War and civil strife damage

Casualty risks resulting from legal liability claims against the exporter because of his actions (e.g., claims by his own or by foreign personnel, product liability claims for marketed goods which are defective or hazardous)

Property risks involving direct damage to assets (e.g., to real property, machinery and equipment, materials), as well as time-dependent exposures (e.g., loss of earnings or increased expenses due to business interruption)

Pure business risks resulting in losses for the exporter (e.g., due to license infringements, loss of competitiveness because of adverse shifts in markets or higher than projected production costs, excessive costs incurred in marketing counterpurchases)

Except for pure business risks, all other forms of risk described above are insurable. Pure business risks also include those resulting from the unfamiliarity and inexperience of many exporters with the identification and realistic evaluation of CA costs, or just due to lack of advance planning. Poor cost estimates related to counterdelivery commitments may result from delays caused by changes in production priorities in a developing country, from the sudden unavailability of domestic feedstocks and materials, or from inadequate transportation facilities. For example, manufacturing scheduled to fulfill counterpurchase commitments has lower priority in the Soviet-bloc countries' production planning than that for exports. Delivery delays of such goods are common, and manufactures or equipment, when not of poor quality, lack after-sale services, adequate packaging, and spares. Thus a western importer may have to keep substantial inventories of the countertraded product and establish his own after-sale service in order to satisfy his marketing requirements.

Delays may also be caused by the tendency of some developing-country production managers to overestimate their ability to perform according to planned production schedules. This could be due to problems in assimilating a new technology, or to environmental or bureaucratic foul-ups, cost overruns, malfunctions due to improper maintenance or installation of equipment, unavailability of materials, or other factors. When the CA involves sales of western machinery and equipment intended to process goods in a developing country on account of the western exporter, the machinery and equipment become the exporter's collateral and a basis of repayment through the delivery of processed goods. An inherent risk is the possibility of production loss due to consistent equipment malfunctions or damage caused by improper use and maintenance. Contractual or insurance coverage for business interruption could help reduce the loss of earnings and incurred expenses.

Another potential cause of business interruption is the way centrally planned economies control allocation and pricing of materials or feedstocks destined to production. The applied criteria may not take into account the interest of individual compensatory contracts with western companies. Even if production feedstocks and materials are made available in fulfillment of CA contractual obligations, their government-fixed prices may become at times noncompetitive with the fluctuating price structure of the same feedstocks and materials on the free markets, resulting in excessive production costs for the CA. For example, the high content of copper used in power switches manufactured by a Chinese plant in Shanghai created a problem in pricing the product competitively as part of a long-term CA involving transfer of western technology. The problem resulted from the fixed price at which copper was made available by the government to the manufacturer of the power switches; given the volatility of copper prices in the international market, this could have made the switches' production costs uncompetitive. For such eventualities, it may be necessary to include in the CA contract a clause specifying the option of the western party to source production materials wherever it may be more cost-effective. Alternatively, the western party may reserve the right to source the finished products elsewhere whenever the counterdeliveries are not competitively priced.

Other risks incurred by western companies engaging in long-term CAs involve potential product-liability claims by purchasers of the counterdelivered goods, higher than projected production costs, and adverse shifts in markets. Also, planned production and marketing goals in centrally planned economies often conflict with the western company's aims of maintaining flexibility in production and marketing so as to conform to changing market conditions. These economies' dedication to steady annual economic growth, which is reflected in the production goals of individual plants and in the mentality of plant managers, fosters an inherently inelastic attitude whenever changes in plant output or production methods are desirable or essential so as to conform to changes in demand. Protection against this eventuality is afforded by appropriate clauses in the CA contract which will assure a degree of flexibility to accommodate changes in market conditions. Because developing-country production managers may overestimate their ability to perform, and in order to avoid unwelcome interruptions in the flow of counterdeliveries, the western exporter involved in a long-term CA contract should make efforts to assure himself of:

The allocation of local resources and materials to the project, and their pricing structure

The availability of adequate local utility resources (e.g., electricity, water), as well as of waste treatment and disposal facilities for future production expansions

The accuracy of domestic-demand data or estimates, and the production plants' commitments, if any, to fulfill such demands

Applicable official regulatory policies and current environmental concerns with the plant's methods of operations

The adequacy of transport from the plant to foreign locations

The managerial and labor skills of the plant's personnel, and local customs for personnel rotation and retention

The record of equipment malfunction, and provisions for repairs and for procuring spares in the host country, particularly for the plant under contract

The record in meeting prescribed production levels and delivery schedules in the host country's industrial sector, or in the plant under contract

The degree to which outside subcontracting is necessary for the manufacture of the finished product to be exported to the western party

In general, it is prudent to apply sound risk-management principles to CAs (as well as any other import or export transaction) and, having identified acceptable risk, to determine its possible treatment through assumable and/or insurable exposure. Table 7 summarizes the main risks associated with trade transactions, including CAs, and suggests possible methods of coverage for the assumed exposures.

Table 7
Methods of Protection against Foreign Transaction Risks

	Method of Protection		
Risk Area	**Preferred Characteristics of Project**	**Contract Clauses**	**Insurance Type**
Political	Host government is stable and has good relations with the western exporter's government Host government participates or manifests serious interest and support for the project Both the exporter's and the importer's governments finance and/or guarantee the project	Contract makes project contingent on approval by governments of both parties Contract provides for limited or incremental asset exposure by exporter	Political risk coverage
Resources	Materials and feedstocks for the project are available in the host country Comparative advantages for production exist Adequate utilities for current and projected production needs are locally available	Contract commits local resources to project Contract provides for multiple sourcing options	
Technical	Technology falls within the importer's range of needs and assimilation capability; i.e., limited training is needed Project upgrades existing production facilities	Contract protects against loss of technology; arbitration is provided in third country Consideration is given in contract to safety and environmental issues	Commercial insurance for property damage, business interruption, and casualty exposures

Table 7
Methods of Protection against Foreign Transaction Risks (*Continued*)

	Method of Protection		
Risk Area	**Preferred Characteristics of Project**	**Contract Clauses**	**Insurance Type**
Technical (*Cont.*)	Project involves partial assembly, processing, or component production	Contract specifies that western exporter will provide critical materials or components, if these are not available locally or do not meet specifications	
Financial	Host government and importer are creditworthy Hard-currency allocations are budgeted, at least for a major portion of the project Project provides for an adequate component of the revenue stream in the currency in which the importer's debt is to be serviced	Contract provides for immediate (prior to project completion) revenue streams derived from host country exports to hedge against negative cash flows; these are assigned either to the western exporter for his own use or to a designated third party, with revenues flowing into a trust account held by a western bank, preferably outside the host country, which segregates the revenue stream and assigns it for import repayment	Political risk and export credit insurance; insurance against currency fluctuations (available in some western countries) and against revocation for the use of export proceeds to service import repayment
Transportation	Host country has adequate transportation networks and facilities	Contract provides for alternative transport options Contract allows options for selecting delivery sites and schedules	Commercial insurance for business-interruption exposure

(Table continues)

Table 7
Methods of Protection against Foreign Transaction Risks (*Continued*)

	Method of Protection		
Risk Area	**Preferred Characteristics of Project**	**Contract Clauses**	**Insurance Type**
Commercial	Steady demand for the counterdelivered products is foreseen; project manufactures goods for use by western exporter Project involves take-or-pay, minimum-payment or deficiency-payment contractual commitments by user(s) of the counterdeliveries*	Contract provides for long-term deliveries at discounted prices; contract provides for flexible production levels to conform to changes in markets Contract provides for quality-control and packaging specifications Contract addresses labor and production issues, as well as local subcontracting requirements	Commercial insurance for business-interruption exposure

*See Chapter 9 for a description of these types of contracts.

The Compensatory Arrangement Contract

The drafting of a CA contract usually requires protracted negotiations, since clear, unambiguous wording of its clauses can avoid subsequent difficulties over the lifetime of the CA obligation. CAs involving coproduction or subcontracting will require the structuring of contracts which will conform to the particular conditions and requirements of the project under consideration and which, in most respects, do not differ from similar contracts used in western countries. Because of the individual nature of this type of contract, we will deal in this section only with countertrade contracts, since their clauses are easier to categorize and because their terms are at times prescribed by the importing country's regulations.

In structuring a direct- or indirect-compensation arrangement, except for barter transactions, it is preferred practice to keep the export contract separate from the related import contract. Two separate contracts allow the flexibility of separate financing and guarantees and insulate the obligations of the two transactions from each other.

Normally, the conditions of the two parallel contracts—if not the details of the countertrade commitment—are negotiated at the same time. The obligations of the western exporter are spelled out in a document called a "frame contract" in Soviet-bloc countries, a "protocol" in the Soviet Union, and a "letter of undertaking" in Indonesia (see examples in Appendix D). This binding document serves as the basis for guidance and referral for subsequent contracts signed by the western exporter—or third parties designated by him—with appropriate organizations in the importer's country, in fulfillment of the countertrade obligations agreed to in the frame contract. A typical countertrade frame contract will deal within its clauses with one or more of the following topics:

Identification of responsible parties and/or a third party designee (usually left unspecified) to whom the countertrade commitment can be transferred (e.g., a trading house)

Cross-reference to the original western export contract

Value of the countertrade obligation expressed as a percentage of the western export contract

Deadlines of the countertrade commitment

Range of products available for counterdelivery and the suppliers or industrial sectors from which they are available; or, the right to link counterpurchases to any goods available in the importer's country

Quality and pricing requirements concerning the counterdeliveries, i.e., as being of "export" standard and offered at "internationally" competitive prices

Conditions relating to transportation and delivery

Right of the western party or his designees to market the countertraded goods in third markets of choice without restrictions by the supplier of the goods who may want to protect his own marketing outlets abroad

Right to choose a neutral surveyor, selected by both parties, to pass a binding judgment on the quality of the countertraded goods in case the concerned western purchaser finds them unacceptable

Right to release the western party unconditionally and without financial claims from that part of his countertrade obligations which is not made available according to contracted time and quality standards

Provision that the contracted countertrade obligation would be legally annulled in case of cancellation of the western export contract

Provision that payment of the penalty for nonfulfillment of the countertrade obligation automatically releases the western party from all further countertrade obligations associated with the western export contract

Provision for separation of the obligations relating to penalties for nonperformance by the western party from the payment obligations of the importer

Adjustments in the western party's countertrade obligations resulting from his claims of force majeure

Seat of the arbitration court and the governing law in case of legal conflicts

Since, obviously, not all the above clauses will be acceptable to the importer, the provisions actually included in the frame contract will depend on the skill and leverage that the western exporter is able to exert during his negotiations.

In fulfilling the countertrade conditions set forth in the frame contract, the western exporter or other parties designated by him will negotiate at some later date one or more purchase contracts in the importer's country. The clauses of these purchase contracts will be compatible with, and will refer to, those spelled out in the frame contract. Developing-country exporters from whom the counterdeliveries are sourced will normally provide the western firms with their approved version of export contracts. Soviet-bloc countries in particular use standardized contract formats covering their counterdelivery commitments which include vague penalty provisions (or even lack them) and which specify arbitration sites in their own countries. Although these countries' exporters prefer to adhere to the format of their standardized contracts, the western firm may negotiate amendments to such contracts to suit its particular needs.

In another communist country, the People's Republic of China, legal formalities are less established. Traditionally, the Chinese have preferred a minimum of legal formalities in business transactions and have no developed body of commercial law. Their circumspect attitude toward the legal profession in general is reflected in the adage; "It is better to enter the tiger's den than a court of law." The traditional and preferred mechanisms for solving disputes are conciliation and, as a last resort, arbitration. Thus contracts, including countertrade ones, have been kept simple and brief (see example in Appendix D), although this practice is now changing as China acquires more experience with western practices.

No penalty provisions affecting the Chinese party are usually included in the contracts covering counterdelivery commitments, beyond vague statements such as one showing a willingness to "indemnify buyers from any loss or damage caused by deviation of quality or specification" (see article 6 of Chinese sample contract in Appendix D). Instead, the advocated mechanism for solving disputes is through "mutual" or "friendly" negotiations. Force majeure provisions, if included in the contracts, are spelled out as, for example, war, flood and earthquakes, strong wind storms, or serious fire. Strikes are not recognized as contingencies beyond human control. Chinese negotiators may also oppose clauses in the countertrade contract relating to quality-control inspections, unless these requests are proved to their satisfaction to be critical to the manufacturing process and the quality of the end product, or unless the presence of foreign inspectors can be justified on the basis of technical assistance related to the improvement in production methods.

From the western exporter's point of view, the careful drafting of contracts is imperative because of the lack of a developed commercial law body in China. Substituting for contract law are the terms of the contract which, once approved, become the only instruments of reference for all future operating decisions and which the Chinese will honor as if they were law. Thus, contract language should not leave room for interpretations and should account for all aspects of the transaction defining the parties' rights, responsibilities, and remedies. In general, western exporters should take into account that countertrade contracts, along with a viably construed and priced commercial transaction and with any insurance available for such deals, represent a major protection against risks that the exporter assumes.

U.S. Trade Laws and Compensatory Arrangements

Existing U.S. statutory law governing trade applies to any imports sold in the United States, whether these imports derive from normal commercial transactions or from a CA. Applicable laws are the Trade Act of 1974 and its market-disruption provisions (sections 201 and 406) and the Tariff Act of 1930 as amended by the Trade Agreements Act of 1979, which sets forth antidumping and countervailing-duty provisions of law.

Section 201 of the Trade Act of 1974 is aimed at providing temporary relief for an industry suffering from serious injury, or the threat thereof, due to import competition. An escape clause permits the American company to petition for import relief, which is intended to allow it to make orderly adjustments, inclusive of transferring resources to alternative uses, which are necessitated by the foreign competition's pressures. Section 406 deals with import restrictions aimed at preventing or remedying market disruption caused by imports. To show market disruption, imports must be in competition with those domestically manufactured, must increase in volume "rapidly, either absolutely or relatively," and must cause, or threaten to cause, significant material injury to the American plaintiffs.

The antidumping statutes of the Tariff Act of 1930, as amended, are intended to provide remedy to unfair price discriminations between different national markets. Under the statutes of the act, imported goods which are sold in the United States at "less than fair value" and which cause or threaten to cause economic injury to a domestic industry, are subject to dumping duties amounting to the price differential between the foreign and equivalent domestic goods. The U.S. Department of Commerce is empowered to determine a "fair value" for the imported goods based on home-market sale price considerations, and if these do not provide an adequate basis for comparison, the department—at its option—may refer to third-country sales or to a "constructed value" based on estimated costs of production, packing, shipping, general expenses, and profit margins.

The countervailing-duty law provisions, also embodied in the Tariff Act, provide for duties to be assessed on foreign imports whenever material injury to a domestic industry can be established as resulting from foreign subsidies to the production, transportation, or sale of the imported goods. The value of the countervailing duty assessed is calculated to offset the effects of subsidy.

Until now, imports related to countertrade arrangements have not been a significant factor in the United States market. The only two federal investigations of countertrade arrangements involved Hungarian truck-trailer axles and Soviet anhydrous ammonia imports. In the former case, it was determined in 1980 that the imported axles were injuring the U.S. domestic industry. The latter case resulted from the long-term agreement between Occidental Petroleum Corporation and the Soviet Union. Under the 20-year multibillion-dollar countertrade arrangement signed in 1973, the American firm contracted to sell annual quantities of phosphate fertilizer and to arrange for the construction of four ammonia plants in the Soviet Union, in return for substantial annual deliveries of ammonia, urea, and potash. In 1979 and again in 1980, the U.S. International Trade Commission issued two separate market-disruption determinations involving the imports of Soviet ammonia derived from the Occidental agreement. In the first investigation, which was prompted by a request by U.S. ammonia producers, the commission determined that market disruption had indeed occurred. The finding was, however, rejected by President Carter as not being in the U.S. economic interest.

Following the Soviet invasion of Afghanistan, President Carter embargoed Occidental's phosphate fertilizer sales to the Soviet Union, along with other U.S. exports, and imposed quotas on Soviet ammonia imports. A new investigation was initiated, in this instance at the President's request, which concluded, however, that no market disruption existed. The case illustrates the adverse exposure to which multibillion-dollar long-term countertrade arrangements may become subject, when market and political conditions change with time.

Concern has been voiced by the Internal Revenue Service that barter arrangements may produce unreported income and by the Customs Bureau that countertrade transactions may result in insufficient import duties being assessed because of the complex nature of such arrangements. Aside from these concerns and the preoccupation in some U.S. government and legislative circles with the potential adverse impacts on the U.S. industry due to military offset agreements involving high-technology coproduction arrangements abroad, the whole issue of countertrade has evoked negative reactions in U.S. official quarters, especially in the context of trade with the Soviet Union and eastern Europe. The attitude stems from the view that countertrade is anticompetitively motivated and coercive, thus alien to the American way of doing business.

While U.S. trade laws may well be adequate to counteract any potential injury to the domestic market caused by the emerging practice of countertrade, their application can be uneven, since current methodologies for evaluation of countertrade subsidies and pricing have not been established and the whole process for determination of injury is slow and costly. It is also true that in a legal-minded society such as in the United States, preventive action and alarmism are readily advocated even before the problem at hand is understood.

A real and new predicament is facing us today in the spread of countertrade practices from the nonmarket economies of the communist countries to those of the third world and even to some industrialized countries. This has increased the complexity of consistent application of U.S. trade laws, not only because of the different lack of transparency that exports from different economic systems might exhibit, but also because of political considerations and the U.S. government's foreign policy preferences, which favor certain countries over others. Whether enough attention and action by the United States will be focused in the following years on the subject of CAs will depend in large part on the degree to which imports related to such arrangements will impact on the U.S. domestic market and on the debt problems of developing countries with which the United States enjoys preferential relations.

chapter

9

Financial Considerations

The methods of financing western exports contracted under a CA do not differ significantly from those which support other, more conventional types of exports. These methods include government-supported credit programs, bank-to-bank credit lines, and supplier or buyer credits. What differs may be the degree of credit analysis and the security or guarantees required before credit will be granted to a CA, especially when revenue streams depend on delayed availability of counterdeliveries.

During the intervening period, the western exporter may have to shoulder negative cash flows due to costs associated with the credit extended to the purchaser as well as to costs he could incur as a consequence of delays in the revenue stream flow of the CA. Financing policies for CAs vary among industrialized countries, with the official export credit agencies of our western competitors following more liberal policies than those of the United States.

Government Export Credits

Government-supported export credit agencies represent the most important source for financing large compensation projects such as turnkey plants, sales of civil aircraft or major ventures such as the proposed 3000-mile natural gas pipeline construction from Siberia to western Europe. Owing to the large value and long-term aspects of such transactions—which may involve credit extension up to 20 years and exposures for hundreds of millions of dollars—only government credit programs may be available to provide the necessary financing and assume the risks for such long maturity periods.

Major government agencies in the industrialized countries provide export support to domestic suppliers through direct loans, guarantees, interest rate subsidies, and insurance programs that provide coverage against one or more risks such as inflation, currency exchange fluctuations, or arbitrary action on bid and performance bonds. These institutions include the U.S. Export-Import Bank; the Japanese Export-Import Bank; the Canadian Export Development Corporation; the United Kingdom's Export Credit Guarantee Department; the Banque Francaise du Commerce Exterieur and the Compagnie Francaise d'Assurance pour le Commerce Exterieur in France; and Hermes Kreditversicherung AG in West Germany. Although these agencies have different procedures for extending credit, they operate in principle under guidelines established by the International Arrangement on Officially Supported Export Credit among OECD governments. The guidelines apply to the lending terms that can be offered by the agencies, and are periodically adjusted. They do not apply to the financing of aircraft and nuclear power plants. In 1983, leading terms ranged according to the per capita income of the borrowing country, from a minimum annual interest rate of 10 percent to a maximum of 12.4 percent, and from a minimum maturity of 2 years to a maximum of 10 years. Despite common agreement, countries occasionally transgress the guideline terms to meet competition from other countries.

The main characteristics of export credit finance, as government credit is also labeled, are that: finance is up to 85 percent of eligible value; the interest rate is fixed and below commercial rates; repayment is in equal, consecutive, semiannual installments and extends over a period which is normally longer (typically 10 to 20 years for capital projects) than that of a commercial loan (up to 10 years); and a grace period of principal repayments may be provided (e.g., when construction is involved). The main disadvantage of export credit finance is the lack of procurement flexibility, since procurements are tied to the country providing the finance.

Involvement by government finance agencies is predicated on supplementing, not competing with, private capital and on the support of incremental exports. Considerations taken into account in the decision to extend official credit include: the eligibility of the borrowing country for the bank's programs; the importance official finance bears for the transaction in view of any competing credit provided by other foreign government finance agencies, as well as in view of the export's availability from other foreign supplies; the projected revenue stream flow and technical viability of the transaction; the creditworthiness of the borrower; the existence of a reasonable assurance of repayment in the form of guarantees by the borrowing country's government bank; and the consequences of the loan on the economy and policies of the lending country.

Although foreign policy considerations play a role in the extension of credit by government finance agencies, these banks have a responsibility to adhere to sound finance practices when extending credit. In evaluating country risk, the finance agency will evaluate the bank's past experience with that nation and the country's political stability and economic profile. Following is a list of economic indicators whose status and trends the banks will scrutinize prior to granting a credit request from a borrowing country:

The gross national product

The trends in the domestic economy due to inflation, employment, and credit problems

The makeup of the country's industry, service, and agriculture sectors

The country's resource and infrastructure development

The national balance of payments

The stability of the country's exchange rate

The country's foreign exchange reserves

The country's external debt and its structure, i.e., concessional, commercial, and official

The country's formal mechanism to service and manage external debt

The country's record of debt servicing

The country's ratio of external debt payments to exports of goods and services

The country's dependency on imports and exports

When the project under consideration involves a countertrade transaction, the banks will have to evaluate the impact of resulting counterdeliveries on the lender's domestic markets, the importance of the transaction in the context of the lending country's foreign relations with the importer's country, the bank's own policies on credit extension to such transactions, and the creditworthiness of the guarantees and recourse provided by the borrower. The bank will need assurance that demand for the project's output exists and will continue to exist in the future at acceptable price levels for the duration of the loan. Lenders also analyze the currency exchange risks pertaining to the financed projects, to avoid problems related to debt servicing in a strong currency and revenue earnings in a weak currency.

Commercial Credit

Commercial bank financing represents the main source for medium-term (5 to 10 years) financing. Loans normally bear a floating rate of interest linked to the London Interbank Offered Rate (LIBOR) or the U.S. prime rate, plus a fixed margin of spread over LIBOR or prime, which is settled upon through negotiations with the customer at the outset of the loan. As lenders are money brokers—i.e., debt rather than equity investors—their fixed rate of return generally represents a small margin over the bank's cost of funds. This negotiated spread over the floating LIBOR or prime rates reflects the borrower's credit standing and the risk evaluation of the project.

Commercial bank financing offers a more flexible alternative than institutional loans (i.e., official credit) in that its drawdown, grace period, and interest rate terms can be tailored to specific projects and the loan is not tied to procurement in the country providing the financing. It has the disadvantage that the interest rate is higher than that of institutional loans and is floating, thus complicating the transaction's economic planning. Commercial bank funding can be:

Bank-to-bank credit

Syndicated credit provided by a group of banks

Credit in support of export credit programs, such as that of the U.S. Export-Import Bank

Credit in support of development bank programs, such as that of the World Bank

On the account of the supplier or buyer of export goods and services.

Apart from funding exports, commercial financing can also be a source for equity, working capital, down payments, local or interest costs, and for any acquisition of assets not covered by export credits. When extending credit on its own account, a western bank will conclude a loan agreement with the importer's bank, say, a foreign trade bank in a developing country. Under these circumstances, a strictly financial claim is created which in most cases is not contingent upon any compensatory provisions such as countertrade.

On some occasions, western banks have financed countertrade transactions by assuming title to the counterdelivered goods as collateral, until these goods were marketed for cash. While commercial banks, unlike merchant banks, frown on such transactions, a major U.S. commercial bank has helped finance a textile plant expansion in the People's Republic of China, which was collateralized—through the endorsement of the bills of lading to the bank—by immediate cotton cloth deliveries from the old plant. In this case, the U.S. company which contracted to expand the Chinese production was also the buyer of the cotton cloth counterdeliveries. The cash derived from the cloth sales was deposited in a trust account held by the U.S. bank and opened in the name of the Chinese contracting party to repay the loan's interest and principal to the bank.

Large U.S. commercial banks, although limited in their U.S. operations by the Glass-Steagall Banking Reform Act of 1933, which excludes commercial banks from investment functions, have nevertheless been increasing the merchant banking activities of their foreign branches and subsidiaries. These banks are also evaluating the options now open to them by the provisions of the new Export Trading Company Act of 1982, which allows limited commercial bank investment in consortia of exporting firms. (See Chapter 10.)

In the case of supplier's credits, the importer will sometimes issue a series of negotiable notes, usually guaranteed by his foreign trade bank or other well-established bank, which carry a fixed interest rate and mature over a medium-term period (normally 3 to 7 years). The supplier can make arrangements with a western commercial bank to discount the notes on either a nonrecourse or a limited recourse (for interest rate changes) basis. The nonrecourse financing procedure is known as *forfaiting*, and will be discussed in the next section. Sometimes the willingness of the supplier to accept bills of exchange or promissory notes in payment, and his ability to find a forfaiter willing to discount them, may avoid countertrade obligations. Unfortunately, the deteriorating creditworthiness of many developing countries has increased the risks of forfaiters and reduced the number of countries whose notes they are willing to discount.

An alternative method of financing is buyer credit. This credit is extended by the bank directly to the buyer in support of an export transaction. As with supplier credits, foreign trade banks may provide a guarantee to such credits in addition to the guarantees provided by the buyer himself. In either supplier or buyer credit agreements, any reference to countertrade obligations is usually avoided, since western banks feel that the repayment of the credit should not be formally made contingent upon counterdeliveries. However, a side letter of understanding may be signed—in addition to the import and export contracts and the financial agreement—that will set forth the agreed-upon reciprocal trade obligations of the parties involved, or the western exporter may open a standby letter of credit in favor of his client to cover the counterdelivery commitment. In other cases, western banks have required that a special account be established in the west in the name of the borrower, into which foreign exchange revenues from the countertrade transaction are placed to service the incurred debt (e.g., the West German steel pipe deal for Soviet gas). Figure 9.1 summarizes the various types of credit discussed in this section.

Forfaiting

With the rapid expansion of competitive international trade in the early 1960s, as seller's markets were changing into buyer's markets, exporters found themselves confronted with demands for extended credit exceeding the traditional 90 or 180 days. As a result, forfaiting was developed as a medium-term refinancing of supplier's credits, using the technique of nonrecourse financing. Practiced first in Zurich, forfaiting then spread to other finance centers of western Europe.

Forfaiting denotes the purchase of trade bills and promissory notes by a financial institution, without recourse to the seller. The trade obligations, arising mostly from export transactions, mature in 1 to 7 years and are bought by the financial institution or forfaiter at discount. The discount relates to the cost of refinancing and includes a

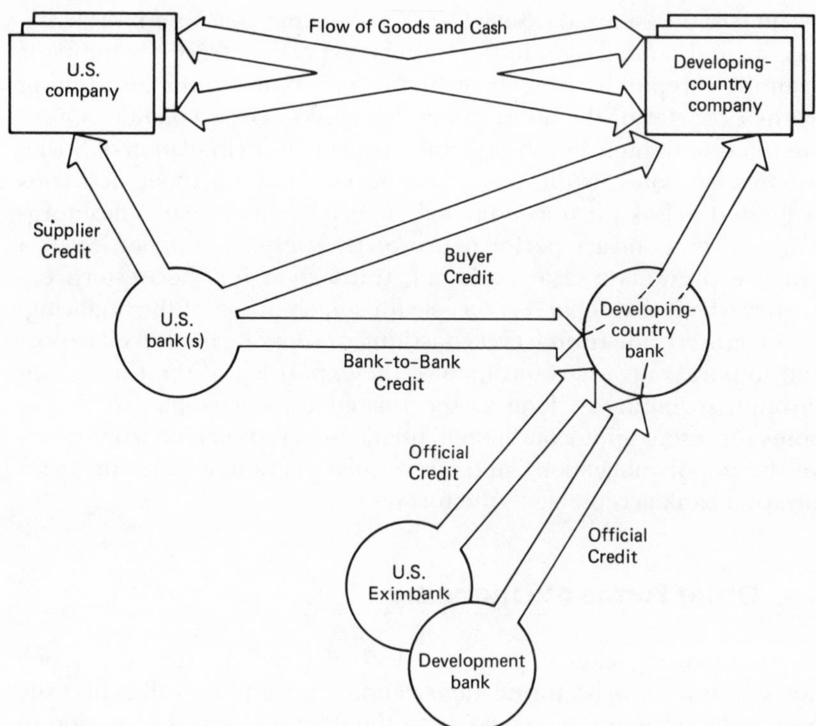

Figure 9.1. Type of credit provided by banks.

margin to cover the risks assumed and the administration of the transaction. Other factors included in the cost are the commitment commission and a "days-of-grace" fee to compensate for the loss of interest due to transfer and payment delays. Discount rates may vary from about 7 to well in excess of 10 percent.

Forfaiting is normally done at fixed interest rates, involving services of notes or bills maturing semiannually. The main currencies used are those of the Euromoney market, but short-term financing for up to 1 year may be possible in other foreign currencies. In most cases, forfaitable claims carry a promise to pay called *per aval*, representing an unconditional, irrevocable, and freely transferable guarantee of payment of a bank—usually the bank of foreign trade in a developing or Soviet-bloc country—or a government agency. The guarantee ensures the free negotiability of the claim, making the risk assumed by the forfaiter a foreign bank or government risk, that is, a political risk if the foreign bank is also a state-run institution.

On past occasions, the Soviet bank of foreign trade, Vneshtorgbank, has insisted on inclusion in the western export contract of conditions granting it repurchase rights or first refusal rights to the discounting by the exporter of the notes to western banks. These conditions were intended to tighten Vneshtorgbank's control over circulation of Soviet promissory notes in the west. The Soviets have on other occasions requested to link the unconditional financial guarantee of Vneshtorgbank to the contract performance of the western supplier. Such a practice prevents a clear forfaiting transaction for the western exporter, who is then held responsible for some portion of the financing.

A countertrade transaction consisting of separate but linked export and import contracts could finance the export leg of the transaction through forfaiting as long as the related trade bills or promissory notes represent an unconditional, unencumbered (i.e., noncontingent on the import obligation), and irrevocable guarantee of payment *per aval* of a bank acceptable to the forfaiter.

Other Forms of Financing

When financing capital projects which depend on future revenue flows or any high-risk transactions, lending institutions will expect the borrowing or guaranteeing party to shoulder a reasonable portion of the exposure through contractual commitments which provide the lender with adequate recourse. For example, the lenders may require the creation of a trust account, based in a western bank or preferably the lending bank, to receive the cash flows derived from the project's revenue stream in sufficient amounts to service debt and meet other essential obligations on a priority basis. Or the lender may provide financing on the basis of the existence of a take-or-pay contract or a minimum-payment contract. Such contracts commit purchasers and users of the output derived from the project to provide contracted amounts or minimum payments sufficient to service debt, even when not receiving or using the output. In capital project financing such as involving the construction of an industrial plant, a creditworthy end user or a government agency or bank may agree to enter into a deficiency-payment agreement whereby the party guarantees to make up any deficiency between the revenues generated by the project and the debt service.

Another form of long-term financing for capital projects is leasing. Leasing obligations appear as contingent liabilities on balance sheets, thus extending the lessee's access to credit. Leasing offers advantages to the lessee because the leased asset is lost or damaged at the lessor's risk; servicing, maintenance, and upgrading of leased assets are the lessor's responsibility; the asset is paid for in regular installments as it produces revenues; and credit ratings for lessees are not as stringent, since they are not purchasing the assets.

In western countries there are significant tax benefits available to the owner of the assets, such as investment tax credit and accelerated depreciation. The portion of these benefits that may be applicable to exports may be passed through to the foreign lessee. On the other hand, leasing is usually a more expensive way to contract the use of an asset, because it involves a middleman—the lessor—and because the transaction's risk is borne by the lessee in the form of the risk premium. Whether lease financing is beneficial to a specific project, especially when it entails a CA, depends on a complex set of economic criteria involving financial, legal, tax, accounting, and acceptable-risk factors (e.g., tied to offshore escrow accounts held in western banks) which are peculiar to individual transactions and have to be evaluated accordingly.

chapter 10

Support Services for Compensatory Trade

Companies facing the prospect of compensatory obligations are confronted with a requirement that many exporting firms, especially the small, medium-sized, and product-specialized ones, are not equipped to handle. Investigations of assistance available outside the company or, alternatively, of other firms' case histories may have relative applicability, as they are peculiar to a time, a product, and a country. They also will prove of limited value unless such investigations supplement and are preceded by substantial homework and review of the company's long-range marketing intentions in export markets.

Why consider compensatory obligations in the first place, and what are some of the risks and benefits involved? A company should assess at an early stage:

The likelihood that CAs will represent a persistent occurrence during coming years in the firm's traditional export markets, and whether the company should bear the loss of CA-related trade opportunities in these markets

The benefit of concluding spot sales which would not occur without acceptance of compensatory demands, against the risk and difficulty of evaluating costs associated with CAs (so as to adjust accordingly the price of exports)

The importance of gaining or maintaining a long-term competitive presence in the targeted export markets, against the time, money, and effort expended in organizing for CAs, and the subsequent commitment to the obligations assumed by such an undertaking

The challenge or necessity to adapt and move with trends in export markets, against the effort needed to readjust the thinking of corporate management

The following pages discuss suggested alternatives and criteria for organizing for CAs and for using supporting services available to the exporter from specialized firms. These suggested criteria, rather than prescribing a formula for dealing with CAs, are intended as general guidelines; they should be examined, adapted, and supplemented by additional considerations so as to fit the specific needs of the exporter.

Preliminary Considerations

Companies which are convinced that today's emerging compensatory requirements will persist and grow in their targeted export markets face alternative options of avoiding these markets altogether; negotiating other concessions which could represent acceptable replacement for the compensatory imposition; or devising steps that would permit them to accede to the demands and handle the assumed obligations profitably. A few chemical companies and commodity trading firms are known to have profited from both the export and the import contracts of countertrade obligations, a feat that in the current trade environment is becoming increasingly difficult to achieve for most exporters. Certain other major producers of consumer goods have undertaken countertrade obligations, along with promotional activities (e.g., cultural exchanges), to penetrate the market with products which rate low in priority in the developing country's imports. These initiatives were taken in the belief that their initial investment would be recouped over a number of years, as their products gain acceptability in the market and the long-term commitment shown is recognized by the importing country's authorities.

However, for the great majority of western exporters, such initiatives are not a practical or affordable approach. These exporters, especially the small, medium-sized, and specialized firms, generally rely on prompt repayments for their exports. They are not equipped to dispose of countertrade goods and are reluctant therefore to accede to such obligations. For these exporters, the choices become either to forgo involvement with the transaction or to determine how much of the assumed obligations could be discharged by the company itself and how much should be transferred to outside parties.

After a corporate determination has been made to involve the company in compensatory transactions, the initial step is to assess the firm's resources which could represent potential assets in such arrangements, especially for countertrade (to which we will mostly refer in this chapter, as it represents a most common form of CA). These assets include: capital availability; type of goods and services exported; trained or trainable personnel to be assigned to manage countertrade transactions; operation plan; and the firm's capacity to discharge on its own countertrade commitments. These five parameters can be applied to the overall export posture of the company or they can be assessed for each product line or product mix exported to a particular country or group of countries. The parameters' significance relative to countertrade is described below.

Capital availability plays an important role in countertrade arrangements, especially when receipt of proceeds from the disposal of counterdeliveries occurs only after the western goods have been exported. During the intervening period, the western exporter may have to shoulder costs associated with the credit extended to the importer, as well as costs that could occur as a consequence of late deliveries of countertrade goods or be related to quality deficiencies. Thus, access to capital for the purpose of concluding transactions involving countertrade commitments and for financing any related unforeseen costs is qualified as an asset.

As for the type of goods and services exported (e.g., to a developing or communist country), any project, product, or technology destined to fulfill major domestic needs or to generate foreign exchange through exports for these countries may dictate little or no countertrade. For example, specialty chemicals and drugs, raw materials, components and most spare parts, or imports destined for priority research projects may require no countertrade. (In the past years, however, some communist countries like Romania have started to press for countertrade obligations for practically all imported goods.) These exports qualify as an asset, since the importer has allocated foreign exchange funds for them and countertrade may be requested only when the cost of the imports exceeds the planned allocations, or it may be routinely asked only as an opening negotiating gambit.

On the other hand, consumer and luxury goods, or any other product, equipment, machinery, or technology for which no foreign exchange outlay has been planned—either because the goods are considered nonessential to the importing country's economy or because they have come to the attention of prospective end users too late to be included in annual purchasing plans—may require 100 percent countertrade arrangements. For example, countries like Brazil and Mexico have issued lists of items for which import approval is granted and for which foreign exchange may be made available. It has been suggested by authorities responsible for import approval into these countries that foreign goods not on the lists might still be exported to the countries on a barter basis, i.e., without any cash flow taking place. Exports falling in the categories described above would represent an asset of little or no value for avoiding countertrade obligations.

In assessing the value of in-house personnel who can be assigned to handle or manage countertrade transactions, the need and costs deemed necessary to upgrade and train such personnel should be taken into consideration, together with costs needed to secure assistance from experts or specialized firms outside the company. The latter could include trading houses, banks, or consulting firms.

In the initial stages of involvement with countertrade, some firms will assign responsibility for developing the company's countertrade programs, or for suggested initial steps, to one of its management officers in sales, procurement, or business development. Many other companies getting involved in countertrade rely on the services of a single salaried specialist, sometimes recruited from the outside, who has a background in trade and marketing involving experience with imports as well as exports. The salaried specialist acts as a coordinator between the sales and purchasing departments, consulting on countertrade activities. His main function is to determine whether or not the countertrade costs will offset the profits derived from the company's sales in its export markets. His trading expertise is expected to assist the company in locating outside buyers, such as end users or trading houses, for countertrade products that cannot be absorbed within the company. When necessary, the specialist may assist in identifying financial institutions that provide credit for countertrade transactions.

Other companies starting in the countertrade field may hire the services of a consultant on a temporary basis. The consultant's responsibilities include advising the company on countertrade policies and planning; the most appropriate organizational structure and guidelines related to countertrade; markets likely to impose such obligations on the company's exports; and, occasionally, countertrade negotiation strategies. Consultants having extensive knowledge of countertrade-related matters are few in number and more difficult to secure than traders or marketing specialists. Any in-house expertise on countertrading or expertise accessible outside the company represents an asset for the firm.

The development of a marketing plan which takes into consideration countertrade as one of the optional recourses is a definite asset for a company expecting to encounter such obligations in its export market. The plan should identify goods potentially available as counterdeliveries by type and quantities, should detail preventive measures, and suggest approaches and strategies, methods and sources of financing, in-house matrix management procedures (i.e., across divisional lines), and logistical requirements. The plan should further recommend to what degree countertrade should be treated as a marketing tool for the enhancement of the company's exports or as a profitable source of supplies. These points were treated in the Chapter 7 discussion on planning for compensatory trade.

Once a western exporter has agreed to countertrade terms, his ability to handle counterdeliveries on his own or through the assistance of third parties is another asset for his company. This could be achieved by absorbing the counterdeliveries within the exporter's company or within those of its clients and subcontractors by having certain products manufactured in the importing country to a western firm's specification and for its own use (e.g., components). The western exporter may also assist the foreign country importer to raise the foreign exchange needed to finance the western exports by identifying export opportunities in foreign markets on behalf of the importer, or he may choose to transfer his countertrade obligations to a broker against payment of a subsidy or premium. Table 8 summarizes the five parameters discussed above.

After a review is made of the company's assets for countertrade—

Table 8
Assets for Countertrade

Parameter	Description
Capital	Availability of financing
Priority imports (e.g., raw materials, components, most spare parts)	Require few or no countertrade obligations, in contrast to consumer goods, which require large countertrade obligations
Expertise	Availability of in-house specialists and outside assistance
Operation plan	Treating countertrade as an export marketing tool to be subsidized or as a profitable source of supplies Identifying logistical requirements and recommending strategies and organizational steps
Capacity to handle counterdeliveries	By absorbing them within the company By placing them with subcontractors By transferring them to brokers

i.e., its current ability to cope with such obligations—the company can decide where improvements are in order and decide on the costs of undertaking them. As a result of the initial assessment, the following alternatives present themselves for consideration:

Engage in countertrade transactions only when it is possible to transfer all such obligations to third parties.

Transfer only some countertrade-related functions or services to third parties—e.g., representation within certain geographical areas.

Organize the company's own in-house countertrade unit.

In the initial stages of involvement with countertrade, many companies prefer to adopt the first alternative rather than assume the risks of marketing the countertrade goods on their own. Even when the established company's policy is to transfer in all instances its assumed countertrade responsibilities to third parties, it is recommended that in-house personnel of the firm be trained to develop the necessary expertise allowing them to selectively secure the best-suited outside assistance on the most favorable terms for their company.

In-House Capability

Companies which face recurring demands for countertrade in their export markets and which decide that the assistance available outside the company through consultants and brokers does not fulfill their long-term needs may be compelled to organize an in-house capability to handle countertrade obligations. A corporate decision to organize a permanent in-house countertrade unit will have to establish the unit's location within the firm's command-and-review chain, delineate its functions and staffing, and determine sources and budget allocations for its operations.

Review Chain. Whether a company comprises one or several product divisions, it is important that the countertrade unit be established at corporate level to oversee and provide expertise, services, and necessary liaison to divisions engaged in countertrade, and that it be given direct responsibility to corporate management. The unit may be assigned line or staff responsibilities according to the functions it is required to perform and the size of the company. The former type of responsibility is usually preferable because it provides added authority to the unit's functions or may allow for incorporating the unit into an existing company division such as sales, international operations, or corporate development.

Incorporating the countertrade unit into, or subordinating it to, the company's purchasing organization might not be the preferred choice, although some multinational firms have initiated their trading functions in their purchasing departments. It is the responsibility of the purchasing office to locate and secure, on a timely basis, deliveries of specific supplies on which the company's production timetable depends. As a result, purchasing may be reluctant to chance shifting from its established suppliers to new unproven ones for the sake of fulfilling countertrade obligations assumed by the sales department. Furthermore, the goods available for countertrade may be finished products and not components, intermediates, unfinished goods, or raw materials of the type and quality sought by a company's purchasing organization. On the other hand, if the company avails itself of large volumes of steady supplies from abroad, the leverage provided by the imports could be used by the purchasing department—during its negotiations for the annual procurements—to offset any countertrade obligations that the company's exports might incur in that country (see *reverse countertrade* discussed in Chapter 3). However, even if such an agreement could be negotiated, it is likely that the supplier would accede to the company's request only for incremental volumes of supplies above the traditional levels of the company's purchases.

The organizational flowcharts in Figures 10.1 and 10.2 illustrate the main representative structure found in a small to medium-sized manufacturing company (i.e., with sales ranging typically from $1 to $50 million) and a larger manufacturing company (i.e., with sales in excess of $50 million), respectively. In the former, the suggested line responsibility of the countertrade unit would be the vice president for sales; in the latter, it would be the president (or senior vice president) for international operations who directly controls all international activities of the company.

Product divisions in many large corporations are organized as separate groups and are assigned domestic and international profit and

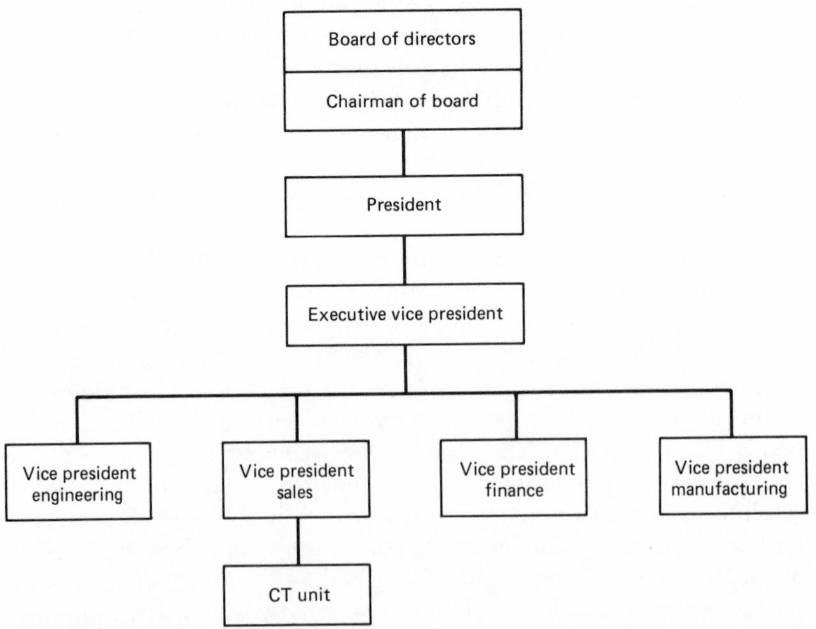

Figure 10.1. Flowchart of functions found in a representative small- to medium-sized firm. Note the suggested line of responsibility for the countertrade unit.

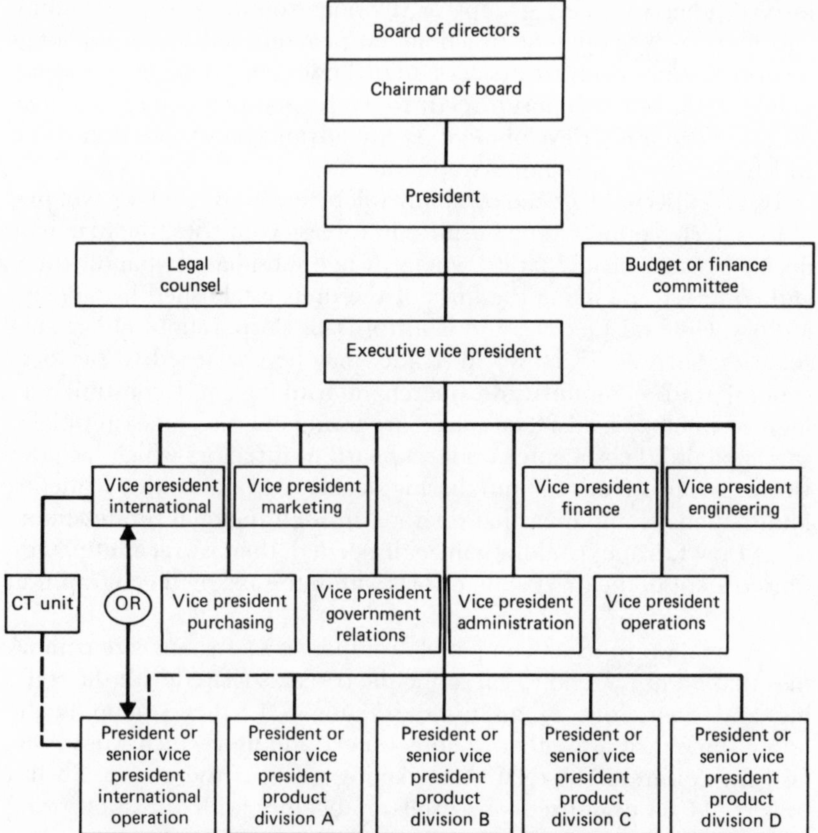

Figure 10.2. Flowchart of functions found in a representative large corporation. Note the suggested line of responsibility for the countertrade unit.

loss responsibilities. The international operations of these independently operating divisions are assisted in their foreign marketing efforts by a corporate vice president international, whose task is to funnel foreign market intelligence to the divisions and provide needed liaison functions with other company units. For corporations organized along the above lines, it is advisable that the countertrade unit be responsible to the international vice president.

Other corporations rely on a senior vice president for corporate development to expand company business in new markets (e.g., the developing or communist countries) and to develop the appropriate strategic planning for sales and technology transfers to these markets. Because it is characteristic of the corporate development group to involve other company groups or divisions routinely in its planning and market-development functions, to propose and argue for long-term (sometimes controversial or unorthodox) approaches to market penetration, and to report directly to the corporation's chief executive officer, corporate development is an advantageous position from which to oversee the countertrade unit.

If it is expected that the company will be involved in a large volume of long-term countertrade business in foreign countries, the firm may decide to establish a separate, wholly owned subsidiary to handle trade and countertrade along the lines of the units established by General Motors, General Electric, and Control Data Corporation. Other subsidiaries, such as Sears World Trade, may be chartered to perform general trade, countertrade, merchant banking, and consulting in high-technology fields. The subsidiary would operate, at least initially, as a capitalized cost center under a board of directors which includes vice presidents from the purchasing, legal, and finance departments. Multinational companies that operate through regional profit centers (e.g., Dow Europe) could organize, if needed, their own countertrade unit to assist in the marketing efforts within the assigned geographical area.

For smaller, product-compatible companies or for any size companies that do not intend to subscribe the costs associated with the staffing and operations of an in-house unit, a further option is the establishment of a jointly owned countertrade unit which would service the countertrade-related marketing goals of the group. Such a unit could be organized—by itself or together with the sponsoring companies—under the Export Trading Act of 1982 (see discussion in this chapter), or it could operate on a shared pro rata cost basis under a long-term contract with the firms subscribing to its operations. Indeed, given the operational costs of in-house units, the problems of integrating their operations with those of other company divisions, and the ever-changing countertrade practices in different parts of the globe requiring increasing assistance from specialized firms (e.g., consultants, trading houses, banks), a small, jointly run countertrade unit could provide participating firms with a cost-effective alternative.

Functions. The undertaking of any countertrade project involves three interdependent areas of activity. These are:

Structuring the transaction so that its costs, potential problems, and realistic returns are identified in the early phases of the project

Financing the transaction by relying on the structuring effort to make it bankable as to the risks and exposures involved

Marketing the counterdeliveries by relying on the structuring effort to identify prospective end users or brokers for the goods, as well as to evaluate the subsidies to be paid to these companies for disposing of the goods

It is evident that the last two areas depend on the first and on the terms hammered out during the project's negotiations. Provided that adequate advance effort has been dedicated to the structuring phase, it then becomes possible to predicate a major part of the project's chances for success on the contribution of this phase, rather than solely on the ability to carry out the marketing of the counterdeliveries. Indeed, in the areas of finance and trade brokering, considerable expertise and services are available today to exporters, while expertise in the area of transaction structuring, i.e., the craft of the feasible in individual situations (especially those related to countertrade), is more difficult to find and less available within most exporting firms. It is in this domain that a countertrade unit may evolve the bulk of its activities in support of the parent company's marketing efforts.

A decision to organize a permanent in-house countertrade unit would involve establishing whether the unit is to have a purely export marketing-support function operating as a cost center, or whether it should serve as a profit center. The former function is the main purpose of most countertrade units, whether operating as divisions or as subsidiaries of companies. A few companies have allowed their countertrade sections to operate as independent subsidiaries, trading on their own account and selling services to other exporters. This permits such a subsidiary to defray any costs incurred by the parent company in subsidizing its operations, but exposes the subsidiary to the risk of fending on its own in a very competitive arena as a newcomer on a block where considerable expertise already exists, and of forgoing the marketing-support function for which the subsidiary was presumably created. Thus a company that designates marketing support as the main function of its countertrade unit's activities should be prepared to fund the unit's operations as a cost center within the company's overall export promotion program.

A countertrade unit established to foster the company's marketing goals and intended to operate through and within the company's existing structure (a recommended initial step) is a service organization supportive of the firm's sales personnel. In its operations, the unit should avoid, whenever possible, duplicating the functions already existing within the company's organizational structure, but should strive to accomplish its goals by working through or with appropriate company divisions. Thus, a clear definition of its mandate and clear delineation of responsibility are imperative to avoid potential difficulties with other company divisions. Following are some typical functions that could be performed by a countertrade unit:

Secure sustained commitment by top management to the company's countertrade programs.

Define manageable risks and limiting conditions acceptable when engaging in countertrade transactions, and set related guidelines for the company's sales force.

Assist with long-range marketing strategy plans in markets requiring or likely to require countertrade obligations, taking into account the countries' changing economic and political conditions as well as the export-related regulatory policies and competitive circumstances in these markets.

Perform an inventory of the company's foreign-sourced supplies, and identify new potential suppliers in countries where countertrade is a factor, to use in fulfillment of the firm's countertrade obligations required by these countries and as leverage for future company exports (reverse countertrade).

Participate in negotiations involving countertrade requirements with (or without) contract authority.

Identify and enlist the necessary support from third parties (potential end users of countertrade goods, brokers, banks) to assist the company with its countertrade commitments on a transaction-by-transaction basis, and act as a one-stop information source within the company for all countertrade-related issues.

Coordinate internal clearing of debits and credits within the company resulting from sales by a division and purchases by another division which offset the former division's countertrade obligations.

Manage cash flows to a subsidy fund endowed by one, several, or all the exporting divisions of the company, which is intended to create an incentive and to subsidize countertrade imports by any division of the company, e.g., the purchase department.

Evaluate expected costs resulting from the company's involvement with countertrade transactions (e.g., interim financing, insurance, and subsidies to brokers).

In mapping a long-range marketing strategy, the countertrade unit will strive to provide flexibility of alternatives for individual export markets, taking into account the markets' peculiarities, economic growth, and any other local conditions. Realizing that acceptance of countertrade demands is but one of the available tools for preserving and enhancing the company's market position, the countertrade unit would recommend to the firm's top management, at various stages of market penetration, alternative marketing approaches spanning direct sales, licensing, coproduction, and joint venture with a local partner or with another foreign firm. Thus it is the growth dynamics and characteristics of the importing country, as assessed by the countertrade unit, that condition the evolving marketing strategy of the company, rather than individual, uncoordinated initiatives by any of its divisions, including those of any trading subsidiary.

During the first years of operation and while the company's experience with countertrade is growing, the unit acts as a buffer, focusing the attention of corporate management onto the countertrade-related predicaments of the firm's business units; it also acts as a catalyst, facilitating strategic conceptual information flows from top down, and concrete and practical information flows from bottom up, as illustrated in Figure 10.3.

Another proposed function for the countertrade unit is to assist management in the development of corporate policies involving the firm's participation in countertrade transactions and to translate these into guidelines for the company's divisions. As experience is accumulated by the product divisions and as they become more self-reliant in

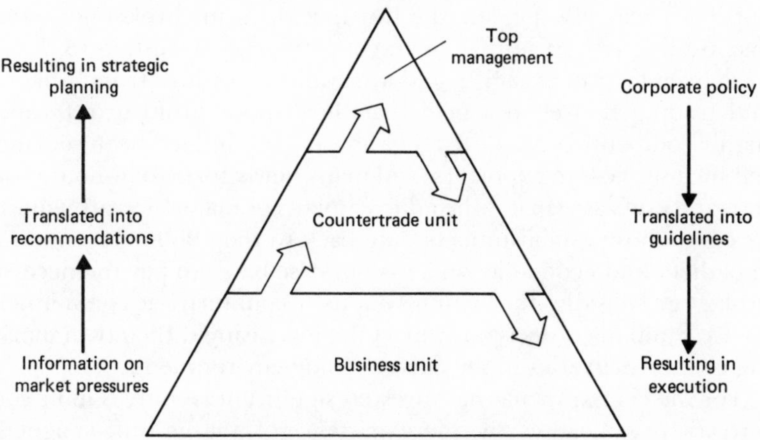

Figure 10.3. Countertrade-related information flow within a company.

conducting countertrade transactions, the role of the unit would gradually shift from overseeing and actively participating in such transactions, to providing only requested support services, information, and liaison with outside firms, which can, on a case-by-case basis, assist the company with the handling of individual countertrade commitments.

Staffing. Depending on the company's size, its degree of involvement in export markets that require countertrade obligations, and the functions assigned, the countertrade unit's staff may range from one or a few professionals in some firms, to tens of specialists in a trading subsidiary. Other factors affecting the size of the unit are its operations costs and any logistical problems related to integrating the activities of the unit with those of other divisions within the company. A small unit with close ties to top management and limited, well-delineated export-support service responsibilities may be easier to integrate with other divisions operating on a profit-and-loss basis than would be a new trading group with contract authority control over the latter divisions.

Some countertrade subsidiaries have indeed been formed by major western companies, involving considerable investment of resources, as an extension of the parent companies' sales and purchasing departments, in the belief that countertrade is akin to trade. Such an assumption overlooks the fact that in trading transactions, supply and demand conditions prevail, while in countertrade transactions only excess, unmarketable supply is most often the norm. The self-reliant approach may also neglect the fact that the same brokerage services and trading expertise that these companies are investing to develop have been long in existence and are available for hire from brokerage and trading houses in a field that shows poor profit growth and is highly competitive. Major trading houses have indeed been seeking to sell such services to exporters, and many newly formed in-house countertrade units as well as offset departments of major aircraft manufacturers—whose establishments date back to the 1960s—are finding it expedient and economic, on a case-by-case basis, to pay the necessary brokerage subsidies for farming out their countertrade commitments. These companies' decisions reflect the increasing difficulty in marketing counterdeliveries in the current trade environment.

For the company that has invested significant resources in its countertrade organization, the mere existence of a large staff assigned to handle such transactions may be an invitation to developing countries to press for countertrade demands. It may also provide a false sense of security to company sales forces who accede to countertrade commitments in the belief that the countertrade unit is able to fulfill them, resulting in a multiplication of such transactions being proposed to the unit. As a consequence, a major portion of the unit's time would be dedicated to running down dubious opportunities and not in providing preventive guidance or in developing market-penetration strategies. On the other hand, if the unit is underutilized because of overstaffing or if operations costs become a concern to the company's management, the unit's expected reaction will likely be to seek out and generate business by engaging in activities unrelated to the company's export efforts (e.g., trading on its own account, selling services outside the parent company) in order to defray overhead costs and justify its existence. Thus, establishing precise criteria and guidelines for the unit's functions (see discussion in the previous section) prior to its formation could impose the desired limitations on the size of its staff, especially if one of the guidelines is reliance on outside assistance whenever it is feasible and cost-effective.

The type of expertise a company would want to secure for its countertrade unit will also depend on the functions assigned to it. Expertise of sales personnel may be too limited, and that of commodity brokers or traders too specialized, for dealing with the evolving dynamics of countertrade practices in various areas of the globe. Rather, a useful expertise is one which emphasizes an ability for planning, i.e., one that can translate current and predicted market pressures into creative options of marketing strategies suited to the company's products and to the target market's requirements. Such expertise—when coupled to the capability to identify third party assistance which is best-suited to individual transactions, and when supplemented by the product division's own marketing expertise—could provide the basis for the small-size, flexible, and cost-effective unit the company needs in handling its countertrade commitments.

To accomplish the countertrade unit's goal of in-house cooperation, that is, of working through and in support of the firm's other divisions, it is preferable that the unit be headed by a veteran executive of the firm and that its operations be overseen by a board comprising representatives of other departments (e.g., purchasing, legal, finance, and sales). The head executive, in turn, could rely for the countertrade unit's operations on the services of one or more hand-picked specialists who could be hired from inside and outside the firm, or, in the case of smaller firms, on the part-time services of consultants and trading specialists.

Budget. The size of the budget allocated to the operations of the countertrade unit depends on the unit's size, the salaries of its personnel, and the range of activities they engage in. For the largest firms it can easily run into the hundreds of thousands of dollars and become a ready cross section for unwanted attention by the officers of the firm's other operating units, especially if the services provided by the countertrade unit do not rise to all the expectations of those for whom the services are intended. In the initial phase of operations, most countertrade units are line budget items funded as part of the company's corporate overhead, and even after years of operation, most units still continue to be subsidized by their companies as break-even conditions take a long time to achieve.

Funding countertrade units directly by divisions operating on a profit-and-loss basis has not gained acceptance, given the overall "corporate" image associated with the countertrade unit's functions, the typically self-reliant attitudes of many operational divisions, and the difficulty of pricing the unit's services over long spans, laden with uncertain outcomes, of most countertrade transactions. A concept that has been investigated is the creation of a special fund endowed by the company or, in some cases, by the company's profit-and-loss operational units, which would provide the necessary incentive—in the form of a subsidy—to any company division willing to fulfill through purchases another division's countertrade obligations. At present, while countertrade requirements are obligatory in relatively few foreign markets, the problems of allocating substantial budgets to countertrade activities or devising alternative funding sources from within the company are still concerns on which only relatively few exporters are focusing their attention.

The Trading House

Companies that do not contemplate involvement with countertrade on a regular basis or are just starting in the countertrade field may turn to the services of trade consultants or trading houses. Trading house involvement may range from providing advice on countertrade practices in developing countries and assistance during negotiations, to acting as brokers or principals in countertrade transactions.

Trading houses thrive on market anomalies and on the free flow and availability of goods which they secure from their own established market positions and handle through their international marketing networks. Since manufacturing is seldom a major function of western

European or American trading houses, the goods' origin does not concern them as long as these goods are marketable. A trading house will therefore consider countertrade transactions as alternative sources of supply, provided that the countertrade goods can be sold, that their volume does not disrupt the trading house's own commodity or product flows, that adequate profit margins are provided, and that the value of the transaction is above the house's lower limit.

There are several hundred trading houses in the commercial centers of western Europe, Japan, and the United States. Most of these are firms consisting of a few people who specialize in a certain range of commodities or by geographical area. Probably less than 30 major trading houses in the world conduct large-scale operations which encompass multiple commodities, products, and geographical areas. Among the largest are the Japanese *sogo shosha*—nine major general trading companies accounting together for over $300 billion in annual sales, which are supported by over 80,000 employees worldwide and a network of 1050 offices overseas. There are four basic functions that can be performed by trading houses. These are marketing, including representation; transportation, including warehousing and insurance; finance, including investment management and credit extension; and manufacture, including upgrading of commodities. (See Table 9.)

European and American trading houses tend to specialize in one or more of the above, while Japanese *sogo shosha* generally specialize in all four. Involvement by trading houses in more than one of the functions allows them to register an overall net profit on a transaction,

Table 9
Basic Functions Performed by Trading Houses

Function	Assets
Marketing, including representation	Market position and commercial intelligence network. Worldwide staffing of specialists.
Transportation, including warehousing and insurance	Ability to handle large volumes of merchandise on low profit margins.
Finance, including investment management and credit extension	Untied lines of credit.
Manufacture, including upgrading of commodities	Return on equity usually higher than margins derived from marketing activities.

even when they may operate marginally in one of the functional areas. A trading house's main assets are its specialists, financial resources, established market positions, and international marketing network. As middlemen operating in a competitive environment, trading house brokerage margins must remain small; thus the houses rely on large sales volumes and on favorable acquisition price levels (not sale levels) for deriving acceptable incomes. According to individual transactions, trading margins as a percent of sales for bulk shipments may range from a few percent to fractions of 1 percent, requiring that the value of each sale exceeds the million-dollar mark.

In recent years the profit growth of trading houses has deteriorated as their principal products traded come from low-growth and declining industries such as textiles, steel, and machinery or they involve bulk commodities subject to volatile price fluctuations, such as fertilizers, chemicals, minerals, and agricultural goods. For example, Japan's nine major *sogo shosha*'s combined net profit as a percentage of sales dropped below 0.1 percent in 1979–1982, while the firms' net debt amounted to 7 times equity during this period. As a result, trading houses have been looking at ways of diversifying their business and have become receptive to providing services to exporters confronted with countertrade obligations. However, the subsidy requested for handling a client's countertrade goods may exceed the houses' usual sale margins.

Firm commitments to an exporter (rather than commitments on a best-effort basis) to market countertrade goods in low demand whose deliveries extend beyond 1 year may rate subsidies as high as 10 to 15 percent depending on the volumes involved. Such premiums are commensurate with the trader's perception of risk, which must take into account fluctuations in the goods' prices over the delivery span and the securing of market positions against potential competition. The premium requested by the trader may be higher if the exporter's countertrade obligation has to be fulfilled within a short time span as the contracted deadline is close. It will fall likely below the level of the penalty the exporter is committed to pay for nonperformance on his countertrade obligation, as traders expect that the penalty cost has been factored into the exporter's selling price.

Although they are not in the counseling business, trading houses will provide advice to exporters on the type of products that are salable on world markets. If brought in early in the negotiation cycle, the trading houses can assess the market value of the goods offered in countertrade and provide a reasonable estimate on the subsidy or discount required for these goods. This will assist the exporter in preparing the price quotation to his client. On occasion, and if profitable to them, trading houses may succeed in allocating the countertrade obligations of an exporter against their own import accounts, thus reducing or eliminating the countertrade obligation of the exporter.

However, as the number and size of countertrade transactions have increased and the goods offered as counterdeliveries have involved more hard-to-market products, often outside the trading houses' field of specialization, the trading houses are becoming increasingly selective in their involvement in such transactions. Because involvement with another firm's countertrade obligations is peripheral and incidental to the normal commodity transactions of the trading houses, these houses are committing their assets, i.e., their specialists and market positions, only when the returns on their investments are commensurate with the risks of the transactions at hand.

Nevertheless, for exporters who do not intend to participate in countertrade on a regular basis, for those adopting a staged approach in organizing for countertrade, or for companies which are faced with counterdeliveries too large or too varied to be handled by the firms' own means, the benefits of enlisting the services of a reputable trading house should be investigated. Appendix E, which is intended to be illustrative and not comprehensive, lists several of the major international trading houses.

The Banks

Major banks have lately been supplementing their export-related services with countertrade advisory ones, in response to their clients' requests for assistance. There are four main services that banks may perform in this area. They can provide advisory services on countertrade-related issues; they can act as middlemen in matching among their clientele exporters with importers; they may provide credits and guarantees (e.g., penalty clause coverage related to nonfulfillment of the countertrade obligation) in support of a countertrade transaction; and they may manage, on a retainer basis, the client's countertrade transaction by securing the assistance of appropriate brokers and monitoring contracted performances. Practically all bank involvement with countertrade so far has been concentrated in the first two areas of activity. This is so because in the banks' traditional ways of assessing risk, countertrade transactions are classified as risky undertakings, especially in current times when risk assumption is being de-emphasized in the financial community. These traditional assessments of risk relate to receiving assurance of adequate revenue streams from financed transactions to allow for potential recourse (the negative-pledge clause in loan agreements) and depend on the creditworthiness of the parties involved, particularly that of the borrower.

The banks remain focused on unencumbered financial transfers, thus clashing with the conditioned trade practices characteristic of countertrade transactions. Yet, stung by substantial loan exposures and rescheduling pressures in the third world, the banks' interests lie in supporting these nations' exports which help assure the economic viability of the countries and their ability to generate foreign exchange for debt servicing. Major U.S. banks have also been intrigued by the potential new business opportunities that countertrade transactions offer, and are thus looking upon the practices with increasing interest.

Indeed, several commercial banks operating in the United States have established in-house countertrade departments; the early ones being Citibank, Chase Manhattan Bank, European American Bank, and J. Henry Schroder Bank. At present, these departments' activities revolve mostly around advisory services, bringing buyers and sellers together for a fee, processing letters of credit, and providing short-term countertrade financing. Staffing and setting operational guidelines for the countertrade departments have not developed without a certain amount of internal conflict and trials. The bankers' thinking differs from the traders' daring style characterized by the taking of short positions, and the countertrade department staffs have, with a few exceptions (e.g., Bank of America, Security Pacific), come mainly from the banks' own ranks. They seldom include expertise in assessing market values of goods and in evaluation of transportation options or costs; instead, the banks rely on trading houses for assistance in discharging the countertrade obligations of their clients.

Lacking the ability to advise on how best to handle counterdeliveries or lacking the willingness to assume the finance risks of most countertrade transactions proposed by clients, some U.S. banks' efforts are gradually shifting to providing one-stop countertrade management services to exporters for a substantial fee. Under such a contractual arrangement with an exporter, the bank provides consulting and advisory services on the client's countertrade transaction. It may assist him upon request during negotiations; it assumes the responsibility to identify and assign the countertrade goods to a broker; it could guarantee, as part of the package, the exporter's countertrade-related nonperformance penalty clause; and it may also provide short-term financing for the transaction. To hedge on its inability to assess on its own the viability of a countertrade transaction, the bank will rely on the creditworthiness, trade record, and reputation of its client, thus favoring major exporters with established competence in international trade.

Because the entrepreneurial mentality of the trader is alien to the banker's training, and the banker's attitudes are nowadays often too cautious in supporting the exporter's aims, the potentially big banking business involving loans to the third world for capital-intensive projects, such as new factories and mines, will probably have to wait for prospective outside consulting expertise. The required expertise would structure financial investment packages—through appropriate collateralization including countertrade—and integrate the different risk notions of the traders, bankers, and exporters into a commercially viable and bankable project. In time, as banks become more comfortable through experience with countertrade arrangements and are able to combine their traditional expertise in securing funds with an understanding of the traits necessary in trading, they will probably end up dominating the countertrade business. The Export Trading Company Act of 1982, which allows bank holding companies to set up export trading firms, hands banks a unique opportunity to achieve this goal.

The Export Trading Company

The Export Trading Company Act of 1982 (Public Law No. 97–290) was signed into law by President Reagan on October 8, 1982. The legislation's purpose is to increase U.S. exports by liberalizing export finance restrictions, allowing bank holding companies to invest in export trading companies (ETCs), and by mollifying the application of antitrust laws to certain export trade. Rather than specifying a particular form of trading company, the act provides American business with a tool the successful exploitation of which depends on the ingenuity, initiative, and resourcefulness of the participating firms.

Stimulating the act's enactment have been the concern in American government and legislative circles with the steadily burgeoning U.S. trade deficits (from $25 billion in 1980 to over $100 billion in 1984) and the limited involvement by U.S. manufacturers—especially by small and medium-sized companies—with exports. Only about 10 percent of the 250,000 manufacturing firms in the United States export, with fewer than 1 percent of these accounting for 80 percent of exports.

U.S. antitrust laws affecting the formation of cooperative export activities have also been singled out by exporters as putting American business at a competitive disadvantage with foreign firms, along with U.S. banking laws which draw strict lines between banking and commerce. The Glass-Steagall Act generally prohibits American banks from owning shares of stock of corporations, and the Bank Holding Company Act generally prohibits bank holding companies from owning or controlling corporation stocks of any company that is not a bank. The ETC legislation was intended to address and provide a measure of remedy for these problems and restrictions.

The Act. The ETC Act has four titles. Title I contains general provisions including applicable definitions. It defines an ETC as a company doing business in the United States which is "principally" engaged in the export of goods and services produced in the United States or involved in facilitating such exports (e.g., providing consulting, financial, insurance, legal, marketing, transportation services, etc.). The definitions implicitly allow foreign ownership of ETCs and the involvement by ETCs in importation, compensatory trade, and sale arrangements between third countries, as long as export business remains the principal activity of the company. Title I also requires the U.S. Department of Commerce to establish an office to promote and assist interested companies in forming ETCs.

Title II, entitled the "Bank Export Services Act," amends the Bank Holding Company Act of 1956 to permit bank holding companies and other banking institutions to own up to 100 percent of the shares of an ETC upon approval of the Federal Reserve Board. The size of a banking entity's investment is limited to 5 percent of consolidated capital and surplus, while loans to an ETC are restricted (at any one time) to 10 percent of such capital and surplus. Title II also directs the Export-Import Bank to establish a loan-guarantee program for ETCs to be secured by export accounts receivable or inventories of exportable goods, and it liberalizes restrictions on the permissible number of banker acceptances—banks' irrevocable guarantees of payment to sellers—issued by federally regulated banks.

Title III, entitled "Export Trade Certificates of Review," establishes the procedures that a company must follow to apply for a certificate of review from the U.S. Department of Commerce which would exempt it from the application of antitrust laws. To meet the criteria, the applicant must show that his proposed activities will:

Not substantially lessen competition or restrain trade within the United States or substantially restrain the export trade of a competitor

Not unreasonably affect prices of goods or services within the United States of the same class as those exported by the applicant

Not constitute unfair competition against competitors engaged in the export of goods and services of the class exported by the applicant

Not result in the sale for consumption or resale within the United States of the exported goods and services

Once a certificate has been issued, the holder is afforded qualified exemption from criminal and civil antitrust action under U.S. law (not foreign antitrust laws), and is required to submit annual reports to the Department of Commerce in such form and at such time as required. While the Justice Department may sue the holder at any time "to enjoin conduct threatening clear and irreparable harm to the national interest," private antitrust suits are limited only to actual damages—as opposed to treble damages usually awarded under antitrust laws. The filing of a suit has a 2-year statute of limitations from the date of violation notice or, at the most, 4 years from the time the violation has occurred; and a certificate holder is permitted to recover costs for defending a suit brought against him under the act, if the plaintiff fails to establish his violation claim.

Title IV extends and supplements Title III by modifying the antitrust provisions of the Sherman Act and the Federal Trade Commission Act. Entitled "Foreign Trade Antitrust Improvements Act of 1982," Title IV narrows the application of antitrust enforcement to export-related activities that have a "direct, substantial, and reasonably foreseeable effect" on domestic or import commerce, or on export trade of an American exporter. Appendix F summarizes the provisions of the ETC legislation.

Functions of an ETC. The basic functions of an ETC are to aggregate an appropriate mix of resources and to apply them effectively, i.e., profitably, in order to enhance the export capabilities of its members and clients. While the mix and depth of these resources may vary according to the ETC's intended operations, its specialization, and its availability of export-related means, the trading company must possess several fundamental capabilities in order to perform properly:

Access to financial funds, resulting in the ability to extend credit or arrange for credit extension to customers

A staff experienced in international trade and able to carry out sales and distribution functions as well as export-support services (e.g., market research, product promotion, shipping and servicing)

An efficient communication system with access to international market information and domestic export-support services provided by other firms

A product or service that is marketable

Whenever the functions provided by the ETC relate solely to export-support services (e.g., consulting, legal, financial, insurance) and are limited as to variety, it is important that the ETC have the capability and necessary contacts to supplement its own services with those from other sources, according to the requirements of individual transactions. Indeed, clients of a service-oriented ETC will look upon such a company as a one-stop organization that can manage their trade flows and fulfill most of the required intermediary service steps between the exporter and the foreign purchaser. Table 10 lists a series of core functions that may be performed by a manufacture-oriented ETC for its members or clients.

Structure of an ETC. The configuration of an ETC, defined by the range of goods, services, and expertise that its membership contributes, depends upon the purposes to be served. The intent in assembling such an organization may vary from solely providing trade-support services to exporters at large, to fostering the trade of the ETC's own membership. In all cases, the structure of the ETC is dictated by the purpose of matching the trade needs of the suppliers and end users, be they ETC members, client firms in the United States or abroad, or foreign importers. Configurations may take into account:

Geographical criteria, either by sourcing exports from a specific region of the United States or by targeting American exports to particular foreign markets

Product criteria, by trading within a range of different but compatible products, by specializing in exports within specific industrial sectors, by solely providing export-support services, or by engaging in import-export activities involving a broad variety of goods in the manner of a general trading company

Client criteria, by providing services to qualified U.S. exporters who may be clients or the ETC's own members, by forming an ETC for the

Table 10
Characteristic Functions of an Export Trading Company

Market Research and Development	Trade Finance	Trade Flow Management
Market or project analysis and selection; intelligence gathering	Credit risk assessment and related information gathering	Management of product sales, promotion, and distribution
Matching the ETC resources (personnel, technology, products) with market objectives	Preshipment financing Export or project financing	Packaging, labeling, insurance, customs clearance, and preparation of documentation
Assessment of market entry modes and needed support assistance	Distributor financing Billing, collection, and payments management	Overseas shipping and inland transportation
Selection of product-promotion techniques, channels of distribution, and servicing Monitoring and adjustments	Foreign exchange management Risk layoff (insurance and government guarantees) Performance guarantees (bonds or standby letters of credit)	Management of customer services and relations Management of product inventory and spares

sole purpose to engage in a specific joint venture or turnkey project abroad, or by structuring the ETC's membership to match long-term supply needs of foreign importers (e.g., established clients and subsidiaries of U.S. firms abroad whose traditional imports are jeopardized by foreign exchange restrictions)

As can be seen, the options for forming an ETC can be varied and can depend on both the exporter's business purposes and his available resources, as well as on the importer's needs. Table 11 illustrates some possible configurations of ETCs, identifying advantages and disadvantages of each option.

In the preparation of the ETC legislation, much has been made of the similarities in potential activities of ETCs and trading houses such

Table 11
Some Possible ETC Configurations

ETC Membership	Advantages	Disadvantages
U.S. bank and U.S. manufacturers	Provides financial resources to ETC members Exports of some ETC members can be offset by imports of others on a debit/credit basis	Exports are limited to the spectrum of goods provided by the ETC members Need incentives for debit/credit system to function Financial risk is contingent on the ETC members' marketing expertise Potential problem may arise if selective financing of members' exports by the member bank is necessary ETC members may have limited expertise in countertrade or limited ability to absorb counter-deliveries
U.S. bank and U.S. service firms (e.g., transportation, insurance)	Provides an integrated financing and trade-flow management service to the ETC clients Does not have to get involved with the client's countertrade problems	Is dependent on export opportunities created by others Income is limited to service fees
U.S. bank and U.S. trading company	Provides financial resources to the trade broker Avails itself of the import-export expertise and capability of the broker	Broker's specialization may be a limitation Import capability may encourage countertrade requirements

Table 11
Some Possible ETC Configurations (*Continued*)

ETC Membership	Advantages	Disadvantages
	Can handle a large variety of goods and commodities	
U.S. bank and foreign firms (e.g., end users, U.S. subsidiaries abroad, foreign banks)	Provides incentives to the foreign partner to import through the ETC Provides ETC with continued business opportunities May facilitate financing and billing services in the partners' countries Eliminates or decreases marketing costs as ETC sells directly to its members' affiliates	Configuration is tied to specific end users, limiting flexibility Management and control of ETC may present practical problems
U.S. manufacturers, brokers, and service firms (no banks); each member contributes a specified amount of capital to an ETC risk pool managed by a bank which is not affiliated with the ETC	Allows bank to operate within its area of expertise, i.e., managing funds Allows pool of funds to provide interim financing and to be leveraged for additional credit Allows bank to lend to the ETC rather than to individual member firms Allows credit-and-debit relationships for exports and imports Does not require Federal Reserve Board clearance	Requires allocation of funds to the risk pool

as the Japanese *sogo shosha*. For comparison, Table 12 illustrates some basic differences between a general trading company (e.g., a Japanese *sogo shosha*) and a manufacture-oriented ETC. Regardless of the merits of underlying concepts or size considerations of either type of company, it is clear that in the highly competitive, protectionistic, and sluggish world trade environment of the 1980s, both types will have a tough going in securing market positions abroad. This might be particularly true in the case of newcomers to the trading scene, such as ETCs.

In favor of the American alternative is the ETCs' unique combination of flexibility resulting from choice of size, area of operations, and form of assembly; the potential they provide for innovative ap-

Table 12
Some Basic Differences between a Large Trading House and an ETC

Activity Area	Trading House	Export Trading Company
Legal	Operates under existing legislation	Operates under new, untested legislation. Needs government certification.
Organizational	Capabilities span one or more of the following functions: Export and import marketing, including representation Transportation Finance, including investment Manufacture	Predominant functions are: Export marketing Export financing
	Is a global firm organized to trade goods from any country	Is essentially a U.S. firm organized to promote American exports
	Has proven and well-integrated multinational organization with sophisticated marketing and communication networks	Effectiveness of ETCs is dependent on the commonality of goals of its members and on its membership structure

Table 12
Some Basic Differences between a Large Trading House and an ETC (*Continued*)

Activity Area	Trading House	Export Trading Company
	Goal is to import and export	Goal is primarily to export. Most ETCs have limited capability to absorb countertraded goods
Financial	Has untied credit lines	Usually no discretionary lending is available from banks. Financing of individual transactions is reviewed by lending bank
Commercial	Deals mostly in goods from low-growth industries, e.g., commodities, textiles, machinery	Deals mostly in exports of industrial goods and services, inclusive of high-technology exports. Has potential to process or assemble goods abroad
	Has as assets established market positions and a staff of import-export traders	Has usually a staff of export (not import) salesmen
	As middleman, operates on high volume and low profit margins	As principal, operates on higher profit margins
	Is at present increasing its representation functions for client manufacturers	Engages as principal in direct manufacturers' sales
	When not registering profits on both exported and imported goods, may be amenable to register an overall net profit in a market over several trade transactions	Normally requires set profit margins for individual transactions. May have to use and subsidize brokers to market countertraded goods

proaches adaptable to individual trade problems; the opportunity they offer to concentrate exclusively in export-growth areas such as the service and high-technology sectors; and the competitive drive to survive and succeed they breed which is peculiar to newcomers who have to make do on their own wits. In time, as more sophistication and experience is gained by those ETCs which survive the test of the marketplace, these organizations will carve out their own niche of trade specializations—which may complement or compete with those of established trading houses—and in the process will help American business become more competitive in world markets.

Since enactment of the ETC legislation, businesses across the United States have taken steps to create, or have already set up, new export trading houses. These include retailers such as Sears, Roebuck & Co., K-Mart Corp., and J.C. Penney Co.; banks such as Bank America and Los Angeles' Security Pacific; small export associations; management and distributor firms; and port authorities such as that of New York and New Jersey. The new companies' impact on future international trade is, at this time, hard to assess, as there has been so little track record on which to base judgment.

chapter 11

Summary

From the increasing number of transactions, growing media attention, and government and private expressions of concern in the west, it is evident that CAs in international trade have increased in importance. As defined in this text, compensatory transactions are not confined only to tied imports and exports of goods between two parties (countertrade), although such practices represent today a major portion of CAs. They may also refer to any type of asset transfer from the exporter to the importer—as a condition of purchase—that results in tangible and desired benefits for the latter (e.g., domestic-content and subcontracting requirements resulting in lower outlays of foreign exchange for imports and in higher domestic employment). Given the sluggish world trade growth rates and the dim prospects for a return to the open market policies of the 1960s in both developed and developing nations, it is in the broader definition of compensatory transactions that these practices will most likely register expansion, rather than solely in countertrade.

Third world countries, unsuccessful so far in their clamor for a new world economic order that would provide them with preferential financial and technology transfers, and hindered in import expansion by the International Monetary Fund's requirements for austerity as a condition of the lending of funds and by the current commercial credit squeeze, have been looking upon CAs, especially countertrade, as a means to balance incremental imports through offsetting exports. Indeed, in today's buyer's market, CAs are increasingly becoming an accepted option in the planning processes of both the western exporters and the developing countries. This trend is not likely to be reversed in the future, as governments continue to treat international commerce as an extension of national economic policies and prefer to deal with trade competition through bilateral accommodations favoring their own exporters.

Arguing for the longevity of compensatory practices are: the accumulated and growing debt of third world countries, aggravated by the steady strength of the U.S. dollar in which 90 to 95 percent of third world debt is denominated; the credit constraints on additional loans to many of these countries and the mounting number of requests for debt reschedulings; the developing countries' continued need for economic growth, which is dependent on sustained import levels as well as on export expansion in order to service debt and to hedge against mounting unemployment and related domestic political instabilities; and the uneven recovery rates in the industrialized countries, together with protectionist attitudes toward many bulk imports from the third world. The roots of these problems are deeper than any short-lived or tentative world economic recovery could eradicate, especially since social impatience has a shorter time fuse than the typical time constants associated with unfettered market-adjustment processes.

Among the various types of CAs, countertrade practices in particular have received conspicuous attention in the west during recent years. Most developing nations are aware of the inherent limitations of such practices which emphasize the temporary needs of the economies over the orderly, long-term development of selective export positions in individual foreign markets. Yet these countries appear to have accepted these arrangements as means to cope with both the short-term problem of balancing trade and the longer-term problem of penetrating western markets.

Indirect-compensation arrangements have been probably the most troublesome form of countertrade, especially when they involve counterdeliveries from a developing country of finished goods manufactured for its own domestic market consumption. Such transactions seldom stimulate improvements in the efficiency or quality of the developing country's production enterprises. They may saddle western firms with hard-to-market products and disrupt their established supply sources. By stressing exports of lower-quality, off-the-shelf goods resulting from its broad-based industrialization effort, the developing country does not concentrate on manufacturing specific product mixes which could ensure it stable positions in western markets. By not sharing in the marketing risks of these goods alongside the western firms, the country forgoes the development of marketing skills and abdicates control over the destination and pricing of these goods. Yet many third world countries with steadily deteriorating economies and with limited industrial bases have had to rely on light industry manufactures, raw materials, and commodities for indirect-compensation counterdeliveries, although these transactions are becoming increasingly difficult to implement.

Direct-compensation arrangements, whereby counterdeliveries are manufactured using the imported western technology and according to western know-how and specifications, are expected to increase more rapidly, especially when involving the processing and assembly of goods and the manufacturing of components within already existing production capacity. Arrangements involving the erection of new production facilities, although less prevalent under present credit conditions than the former, are looked upon by some countries—by virtue of the extended counterdelivery commitments they entail—as a means of acquiring long-term market outlets abroad and as a useful way of financing a major portion of the project. Direct-compensation arrangements are expected to become the preferred countertrade practice in a majority of transactions, and this will likely accelerate the shift in production locale for many light industry goods or components to the more advanced and stable among the developing countries.

Yet if CAs are to expand in trade with the third world, these countries' authorities will have to overcome major problems faced by western exporters. These range from the counterdeliveries' poor quality standards and delays, to lack of after-sale service and product liability insurance, and to the general reluctance and lack of incentive among most western firms to enter such arrangements. Solutions to operational problems will also have to be addressed by third world authorities. These may include promoting special investment incentives as well as organizing and ensuring the proper operation of compensatory coordinating structures at ministerial levels to facilitate, for example, indirect-compensation linkages of counterdeliveries from the entire spectrum of the country's production. An effective coordinating structure may also go a long way toward providing western suppliers with goods that they can absorb within their own commercial organizations, thus avoiding the need for middlemen.

When organizing for CAs, especially for countertrade, companies will have to take into account the dynamic nature of the practice—a tool intended to subsidize the changing needs of the developing countries' economic growth in times of credit constraints—and they may have to adjust their involvement in the markets accordingly. Such involvement may increasingly include investments of capital in addition to exports and technology transfers to foreign countries, thus entailing higher risks for the exporter. Indeed, as production quality improves and production capacity increases, the prevailing tendency may well be to produce countertrade goods to order for the western exporter, rather than providing him with unrelated products manufactured in the country.

The most challenging area of future application for CAs lies in the financing of major projects which involve requirements for funds in the hundreds or thousands of millions of dollars (e.g., development of mines, industrial complexes, or aircraft sales). Whenever western official and commercial credits represent only a portion of the needed funding, CAs may be expected to make up the balance. For these projects with insufficient funding, advance planning and analysis is crucial, especially when the purchasing country's export profile and its industrialization stage do not allow extensive use of countertrade or of domestic-content production.

The planning would have to entail creative approaches and consider such options as piecing together sources of finance, services, and supplies in different developed and developing countries so as to minimize net outflows of hard currency for the importer; creating foreign exchange income for the importer through satellite projects (e.g., building of hotels catering to foreign tourists); and investing in real estate developments (e.g., building of office space) and in other industries in the importer's country which entail growth potential or which may be specified by the host government to fulfill economic or social priority needs.

The last types of investment would avail themselves of any soft currency received by the exporter in partial payment for his participation in the project. Indeed, if convertible currency credit—which has in recent decades propelled international commerce to current levels—is to remain constrained in trade with third world countries, western exporters and their bankers will have to come up with innovative ideas for using soft currencies, if established trade levels are to be maintained. The western exporters will have to weigh its distaste for such unorthodox options against the benefits it expects to derive from the export projects. Alternatively, it may want to curtail the scope of its exports or shelter its participation by engaging in the transactions as a member of a consortium of companies (e.g., by organizing a project-oriented export trading company).

Large-scale projects undertaken in future years in developing countries will undoubtedly result in a larger responsibility for risk falling on the shoulders of western suppliers. Such transactions will also require the increased availability of government finance, and especially guarantees, from both the supplier's and the customer's countries. Moreover, the transactions may require collateral in the form of trust funds held in western banks for the purpose of sheltering revenue streams derived from the marketing of goods (even if these are unrelated to the project's future output) that the importing country has allocated to create initial funds for the proposed project.

A recent example of intimate government involvement in a major project is Belgium's $350 million cooperation agreement to modernize the People's Republic of China's telephone system. The 15-year agreement involves Belgian exports of 150,000 telephone lines, $12 million in interest-free loans to China, and a equity joint-venture factory in Shanghai which will produce 300,000 digital telephone lines a year. The factory is owned 10 percent by the Belgian government, 30 percent by Bell Telephone Manufacturing Company, the Belgian affiliate of the American company International Telephone and Telegraph, and 60 percent by the Chinese government. The rather uncommon occurrence of a western government assuming a personal equity stake in a developing country denotes the high degree of importance that the Belgian government has assigned to this project and to its potential for Belgian exports. While projects entailing direct equity participation by western governments in third world countries are not the norm, increased western government participation—in the form of credits and especially extended and expanded guarantee programs—is crucial if a selected number of the dormant major projects in developing countries are to be resuscitated in future years, for the benefit of importer and exporter alike.

If the uniform high growth rates of the world economies and of international trade that were experienced prior to the onset of the energy crisis were just a fluke in history, during which wealth was created through the availability of cheap energy and easy credit, then future years will require adjustments and more realistic growth expectations. Provided that the accumulated debt problem of developing nations can be resolved without major repercussions on the international financial system, and that credit will be gradually restored—albeit under more restricted criteria—to support trade to most or all of the world's developing nations, the developing countries will have to live with more stringent constraints on their trade balances than in the past. This implies, however, an ability to supplement financial transfers obtained through trade-related credits with market transfers extracted through countertrade impositions.

Reversing a nation's trade-deficit trend in a short period is a most difficult task to achieve without deleterious effects on the importer's economy. As in the case of national debt or asset management, the implementation of any redressing action may require specialized consulting assistance in the form of compensatory-trade-management services. Such assistance would propose steps to maintain the country's trade balanced within designated limits; for the importer it would identify economic sectors where countertrade is indicated and identify criteria for application; it may specify other forms of compensatory arrangements and the sectors which these should benefit; and it would suggest fiscal and other government-sponsored incentives intended to facilitate export-oriented ventures with foreign participation in the domestic market and abroad. As the need for compensatory-trade-management services increases, it is hoped that the forthcoming assistance—the expertise of which is not rooted in precedents, experience, or established theory—will be up to the task, as the margins of affordable error for a developing nation are small indeed.

Future years will be crucial ones for the survival of the international trade and financial system as it was developed in the post–World War II years. The premise of that system—which is based on the existence of unfettered, profit-oriented flows of goods and capital across national boundaries—is today developing serious shortcomings. Thus, the world's nations will have to come to terms with present realities and adapt past practices to current needs which, for an increasing number of nations, find expression through compensatory impositions.

With all the shortcomings of CAs (i.e., lack of supporting analysis due to a dearth of past references, lack of concern for impacts on foreign trading parties, hurried enforcement aimed at immediate solutions, uneconomic results), they have acquired the status of a market phenomenon. Far from being akin to barter-like bilateral trade practiced before World War II under government-mandated or -abetted arrangements, CAs have the potential to make full use of the international financial system and trade interdependence established since.

Current CAs aim to achieve—albeit sometimes through mandatory, unilateral enforcement—the principles of import austerity recommended by the International Monetary Fund, and to combine them with a country's continued need for economic development. While the adoption of CAs will not by itself alleviate problems created in the past, it could narrow future trade imbalances, encourage investments and technology transfers, and pave the way for trade that, in the absence of credit, could not occur. Indeed, the challenge of the 1980s will lie in devising internationally accepted criteria and in standardizing the application of CAs through multilateral negotiations, so that uniformity and predictability can be restored to international trade along with finance credit.

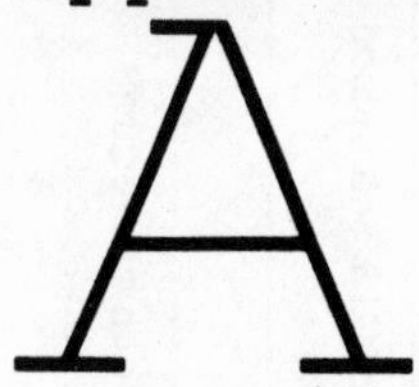

Barter Agreements*

*From Donna U. Vogt et al., *Barter of Agricultural Commodities: IED Staff Report,* U.S. Department of Agriculture, April 1982.

Barter of Agricultural Commodities between Developing Countries

Countries		Time Frame	Commodities Exported		Remarks
A	**B**		**A**	**B**	
Ethiopia	Algeria	3-yr annual renewal	Coffee, hides and skins, oilseeds, spices, and other agricultural products	Industrial products	No specific quantity given First trade agreement between these two countries Signed at ministerial level
Venezuela	Argentina	1976	150,000 mt iron ore	20,000 mt wheat; 100,000 mt grain, sorghum, or corn	Prices to be established prior to each monthly shipment Argentina will pay for the rest in cash Shipments were delayed due to logistics problems
Peru	Argentina	1976–78	Copper, iron ore, cotton	Wheat, corn, beef, offal	Value equalled U.S. $150 million
Peru	Hungary	1977–80	Fishmeal, cotton, coffee, minerals	Wheat, equipment	Value equals U.S. $40 million
Peru	Brazil	1977–80	Minerals, fishmeal	Soybeans	
Democratic Republic of Germany	Brazil	1981–83	Soybeans and products	Coal, potash	Value on each side equals U.S. $100 million
Mexico	U.S.S.R.	Started Jan. 1981 with no time limit	Coffee, cocoa, lettuce	Petroleum extracting equipment, textile industrial equipment, agricultural tractors	This agreement may be a triangle trade pact with agricultural commodities going to Cuba and the U.S.S.R. sending the equipment to Spain and, in the end, swapping customers.

Egypt	USSR	1962–81 annual renewal	Oranges, rice, jasmine paste, wine, shoes, household items	Paper, wood, metals, industrial machinery	The commodity composition has changed as Egypt shifted to cash markets for cotton; substituting other items has prevented a slide in the agreement's value.
Thailand	USSR	12/17/81	100,000 mt corn	Fertilizer	Prices for corn are about $109 per mt and fertilizer $210 per mt. Discussed bartering 300,000 mt corn for 150,000 mt fertilizer.
Thailand	Romania	12/25/81, March 1982 to June 1982	200,000 mt corn	123,834 mt fertilizer	Corn priced at $109 per mt Composition 16-20-0 or 20-20-0 at $210 per mt To be delivered between March 5 and April 30, 1982
Bangladesh	Bhutan	9/8/80	Dried fish, newsprint, jute and jute products	Forest products and stone boulders	Trade agreement. Signing had been delayed almost 2 years because of Indian displeasure over the agreement. The agreement is of greater interest to Bhutan because the country is eager to reduce dependence on India and contributes to strengthening ties with other small countries of the region.

Note: mt = metric ton.

Barter of Agricultural Commodities between Developing Countries (*Continued*)

Countries		Time Frame	Commodities Exported		Remarks
A	B		A	B	
Zambia	Zimbabwe	One-time transaction	10,000 mt cottonseed (cottonseed cake)	2,500 mt cottonseed oil	Barter agreement awaits purchase of machinery by Zimbabwe. Zimbabwe will keep the cotton seed meal in payment for crushing the seeds and will return the oil to Zambia. No foreign exchange involved. Each country will pay transport costs within their boundaries.
India	Uganda	Nov. 81 to Nov. 83	Spices, pepper, cardamom, oilcakes, cotton	Phosphates, superphosphates	Goods into both countries will be accorded most-favored-nation treatment. Simultaneously the two countries signed a memorandum of understanding providing for technical assistance in agriculture from India to Uganda.
Bangladesh	Pakistan	2/8/82 March 1982 to May 1982	Jute, agricultural goods	100,000 mt rice	Over half of the rice has been paid for by Bangladesh exports; a small amount of cash may be involved in the end with no interest charge. Another source has stated agreement calls for Sindi rice 40 to 45% broken, in bags, \$250 to \$255 FOB Karachi.

Note: mt = metric ton.

Bangladesh Barter Agreements

Countries		Time Frame	Commodities Exported		Remarks
A	B		A	B	
Bangladesh	Czechoslovakia	9/21/77, 1977–78 (July–June)	Jute, jute goods, tea, hides and skins, specialized textiles, electrical cables, telephone cables, glycerine, cellophane, newsprint and paper products, molasses, ready-made garments	Electrical equipment and accessories, ball and roller bearings, chemicals and dyes, sulphur, scientific hospital and laboratory equipment	Fourth Bangladesh-Czechoslovakia Barter Trade Protocol. Exchange of commodities $5.6 million each way. Exports from Bangladesh consist of 49% jute and jute goods and 51% nonjute products.
Bangladesh	Poland	9/24/77, 1977–78	Jute, jute goods, tea, hides and skins, oil cake, oil bran, cables, specialized textiles, rayon yarn, crushed bone, molasses, handicraft paper and paper products	Corrugated iron sheets, dyes and chemicals, triple superphosphate, electrical equipment and accessories, tools and workshop equipment, sulphur	Third Bangladesh-Poland Barter Trade Protocol. Exchange of commodities $12.9 million in each direction. Exports from Bangladesh consist of 46% jute and jute goods and 54% nonjute products.
Bangladesh	North Korea	11/28/78 1 yr	Raw jute, jute goods, leather and leather products, newsprint, paper, sugar, soap and detergents, enameled copper wire	Cement, pig iron, coal magnesia clinker, mild steel billets	Second Bangladesh–North Korea Trade Protocol. Exchange of commodities amounted to approximately $6,536,000 each way.
Bangladesh	People's Republic of China	12/10/79, 1980–81	Jute, jute goods, sugar, newsprint, paper and pulp, leather, timber, particle board, hardboard, rayon, cellophane	Cement, coal, mild steel billets, pig iron, light machinery, tools	Third Bangladesh-China Barter Trade Protocol. Exchange of commodities $25 million each way.

Bangladesh Barter Agreements (*Continued*)

Countries		Time Frame	Commodities Exported		Remarks
A	B		A	B	
Bangladesh	Romania	10/30/78, 1978–79	Raw jute, jute goods, tanned and semitanned leather, loose and packet tea, newsprint, viscose and rayon yarn, writing and printing paper, cottage industry products, towels, curtain cloth, handicrafts, coir fiber timber, tobacco, drugs and medicine	Mineral oils, soda ash, fertilizers, ball and roller bearings, diesel engines, spare parts for ambulances, tools and workshop equipment, diesel garbage trucks	Fifth Bangladesh-Romania Barter Trade Protocol. Exchange of commodities $7.5 million each way.
Bangladesh	Bulgaria	8/20/79, 1980–81	Raw jute, jute goods, leather and leather products, loose and packet tea, ready-made garments, specialized textiles, crushed bones, wires and cables, coir fibers, handicrafts, hardboards, particle boards and cutlery, rayon yarn, gib pipes, safety matches, super enameled copper wires	Pig iron, mild steel billets, iron sheets, hot and cold rolled steel strips, electrical equipment, copper, zinc, tin plates, transmitters, forklift trucks, soda ash, pharmaceutical raw materials, medicines, veterinary medicines	Seventh Bangladesh-Bulgaria Barter Trade Protocol. Exchange of commodities $10 or $11 million each way

appendix

B

Agreement between the Government of the United States and the Government of Jamaica for the Barter of Bauxite for Agricultural Commodities*

*From Donna V. Vogt, *U.S. Government International Barter*, Congressional Research Service Report No. 83-211 ENR, December 6, 1983, p. 99.

This Agreement is hereby entered into this 25th day of February 1982, by and between the Government of Jamaica represented by the Bauxite and Alumina Trading Company Ltd. (hereinafter called BATCO) and the Government of the United States represented by the Commodity Credit Corporation, an agency and instrumentality of the United States within the Department of Agriculture (hereinafter called the "CCC").
WITNESSETH:
Whereas, BATCO desires to enter into a barter arrangement with CCC under which BATCO agrees to sell to CCC 400,000 Long Dry Tons (LDT) of metal grade bauxite;
Whereas, CCC desires to enter into a barter arrangement with BATCO under which CCC agrees to sell to BATCO 7,238 metric tons of nonfat dry milk and 1,905 metric tons of anhydrous milkfat;
Now therefore, CCC and BATCO agree as follows:

Part A: BAUXITE PROVISIONS

Article I: Purpose

This Agreement represents a portion of a total transaction between the Government of the United States of America and the Government of Jamaica for acquisition of 1,600,000 Long Dry Tons (LDT) of metal grade bauxite for the National Defense Stockpile. The principal purpose of this Agreement is to define the terms and conditions under which BATCO will sell 400,000 LDT of metal grade bauxite to CCC and the terms and conditions under which CCC will sell 7,238 metric tons of nonfat dry milk and 1,905 metric tons of anhydrous milkfat to BATCO. The balance of the bauxite (1,200,000 LDT) will be covered in an agreement between the United States General Services Administration (GSA) and BATCO, which agreement will also contain provisions covering the transportation costs for the 400,000 LDT of bauxite covered by this Agreement. The total amount of bauxite to be acquired by CCC and GSA is 1.6 million tons, all of which is to be delivered prior to September 30, 1982.

Article II: Material

2.1 MATERIAL

BATCO will furnish the management, labor, facilities, materials, tools and equipment and do all things necessary and/or incidental to performance of the work described below:

Item 1 - Provide 400,000 LDT of Grade 2 metal grade bauxite conforming to the chemical and physical requirements of National Stockpile Purchase Specification P-5b-R, dated December 15, 1981 (referred to herein as "Specification"), except that in Article II, Paragraph A, the following is deleted:

Ferric Oxide	Max: 20.0
Titanium Dioxide	Max: 2.5

and the following is substituted:

Ferric Oxide	Max: 22.0
Titanium Dioxide	Max: 3.0

and Article II, Paragraph B, is deleted in its entirety.

Item 2 - Deliver the material listed in Item 1 to the U.S. Government Storage Track No. 10 which is located on the Reynolds Metals Company facilities, Gregory, Texas.

Item 3 - Build, trim and shape the pile of material delivered under Item 2 to conform to the following requirements:

a. Toes of the piles shall not extend beyond the prepared pad on Storage Track No. 10.

b. Outside slope of the pile shall average 30 degrees, but must not exceed 35 degrees.

c. The stockpile shall be built in lifts of a maximum of three feet per lift. The haul trucks will be dumped and dumped material graded with a dozer to form the lift. This method should achieve a density of at least 81 pounds per cubic feet.

d. A berm four feet high shall be provided around the top edge. The bauxite used for forming this berm shall be moistened, compacted and formed up on the inside face to a maximum angle of repose.

Item 4 - Provide a sampling platform located adjacent to the scale used for weighing the bauxite. The platform shall include a ramp or catwalk in order to provide the sampler access to the bauxite in the trucks. The sample shall be taken after the truck gross weight is recorded and before the material is unloaded. The platform and access ramp shall be constructed so as to accommodate various size trucks, and still provide safety for the sampler while being suitable for the purpose of sampling. A drawing of the platform shall be supplied to GSA for comment prior to construction. The platform shall be operational prior to commencement of deliveries.

Item 5 - Refurnish and maintain existing weighing station adjacent to the storage site. The scales shall be certified by a recognized scale company or State Weights and Measures Authority, at least every three (3) months or after major repairs to the scale.

ARTICLE III: DELIVERY OF THE MATERIAL

3.1 SCHEDULE

Deliveries of the material shall begin on or about July 15, 1982, and be completed by September 30, 1982. A minimum of 150,000 LDTs to a maximum of 250,000 LDTs shall be delivered within each 30-day period beginning with the first delivery date.

3.2 DESTINATION

Material will be delivered to U.S. Government Storage Track No. 10, at Reynolds Metals Company facilities, Gregory, Texas.

3.3 NOTICE

BATCO shall notify CCC, or its authorized representative (for Part A of this Agreement, the authorized representative shall be the General Services Administration, hereinafter called "GSA"), in writing not less than ten (10) working days prior to commencement of initial delivery. GSA shall be notified in writing five days prior to any foreseeable and subsequent reinstatement of delivery.

ARTICLE IV: INSPECTION, SAMPLING, ANALYSIS, WEIGHING AND ACCEPTANCE

4.1 LOT SIZE

For the purpose of weighing, inspection, sampling, and analysis, a lot shall constitute 10,000 Long Wet Tons consecutively delivered.

4.2 INSPECTION

Inspection of the bauxite shall be performed or witnessed by a GSA representative at Gregory, Texas.

4.3 SAMPLING AND ANALYSIS

GSA will sample the bauxite at Gregory, Texas. Sampling and sample preparation shall be at the direction and expense of GSA. Sampling shall be accomplished as close as possible to the time of weighing of the bauxite at Gregory, Texas. Representative samples shall be taken from each lot. Samples taken shall be for the purpose of determining conformance of the lot to the requirements of the Specification. Procedures and methodology for the laboratory testing shall be those described in Exhibit A-2.

4.4 MOISTURE CONTENT DETERMINATION

One portion of the sample taken for moisture determination will be delivered to Reynolds Metals Company. One or two portions of the GSA sample shall be used for moisture content determination. The GSA sample shall be dried at a temperature of 140 degrees centigrade for not less than eight hours or to constant weight. The loss of weight shall be regarded as moisture. The percentage of moisture in the sample shall be subtracted from the net wet weight of the lot as determined in Paragraph 4.6 below, and the resulting dry weight shall be used as the basis for payment. The moisture determination of the GSA analysis shall be final on all deliveries and not subject to umpire.

4.5 UMPIRE LABORATORY PROCEDURE

BATCO may request that a sample be sent to umpire for chemical analysis of any compound failing GSA test analysis. The umpire laboratory shall be mutually acceptable to both BATCO and GSA. The average of the umpire analysis results and the results of either GSA or BATCO analysis, whichever is closer to the umpire results, shall be final and govern. For individual lots not in conformance with the Specification, only compounds that failed to meet the Specification requirements may be analyzed by the umpire. The cost of the umpire will be for the account of the party whose analysis is the farthest from umpire's results. If both are of equal difference from the umpire, the cost will be shared equally.

4.6 WEIGHING

Weighing shall be performed by an official weighmaster mutually acceptable to GSA and BATCO at the Reynolds truck scales located as close as possible to the storage site. Weighing shall be at the expense of GSA. Every truck shall be gross weighed prior to delivery of the bauxite to the storage area. The tare weights of the trucks shall be established periodically as directed by GSA. A complete record of weights by scale weight tickets shall be made for each vehicle for each load hauled. Weight certificates listing truck weight data in tabular form shall be issued by the weighmaster. When a completed lot of material has been weighed, a certified weight certificate shall be signed by the weighmaster and attested to by the GSA representative.

4.7 ACCEPTANCE

4.7.1 If the analysis of the GSA sample indicates that the bauxite complies with the requirements of the Specification when considered on a weighted average basis with all previous deliveries, the lot shall be accepted.

4.7.2 If any lot fails to comply with the requirements of the Specification when considered on a weighted average basis with all previous deliveries, acceptance shall not be made for such lot until (by subsequent lots) the weighted average of all lots delivered shall comply with the requirements of the Specification.

4.7.3 If after 80 percent of the material has been delivered to the site, the weighted average analysis as defined in 4.7.1 does not comply with the Specification, all further deliveries shall cease until BATCO can show that the remaining 20 percent of the material will be of such quality as to bring the weighted average analysis of the site into compliance with the Specification.

4.7.4 The Notice of Inspection, GSA Form 308-A, shall be issued by GSA after receipt of reports on analysis, weighing, and physical requirements on one or more lots. Acceptance or notice of noncompliance of the material tendered shall be made by GSA on Form 308-A.

ARTICLE V: CONSIDERATION AND PAYMENT FOR THE BAUXITE

5.1 UNIT PRICE AND AMOUNT

BATCO will be paid as follows for the bauxite delivered to CCC.

Description	*Quantity*	*Unit Price*	*Total Value*
Bauxite	400,000 LDT	U.S. $32.50 Per LDT	U.S. $13,000,000

5.2 TRANSPORTATION, HANDLING AND DELIVERY TO THE PILE

BATCO will be paid by GSA for the transportation, handling and delivery to the pile of the bauxite purchased by CCC at the rates provided in Article VI, paragraph 6.2, and Article X of the Memorandum of Agreement. Between the Government of the United States and the Government of Jamaica for the Acquisition of Bauxite.

5.3 PAYMENT

Payment for the value of the bauxite delivered to CCC, excluding the cost of transportation, handling and delivery to the pile, as provided in paragraph 5.2, shall be paid for by CCC by delivery to BATCO of an equivalent value of agricultural commodities as specified in Articles VII and VIII.

5.4 BARTER ACCOUNT

Upon delivery to and acceptance of the bauxite by GSA, the value of the bauxite accepted shall be credited to a "barter account" for BATCO. The value of each lot will be credited to the account upon determination of acceptance by GSA, as demonstrated by the issuance of a GSA Form 308-A. The "barter account" will be liquidated as specified in Article XII, by applying to the account the value of the agricultural commodities delivered to BATCO in accordance with Part B of this Agreement.

5.5 INVOICES

5.5.1 An invoice shall be submitted weekly by BATCO to GSA covering the quantity of material to be delivered in the following week. The format shall be one acceptable to GSA.

5.5.2 *Fixed Price*: The unit price of the bauxite as provided in paragraph 5.1 is inclusive of all costs of performance, including costs and cost escalations not known or not contemplated at the time this Agreement was signed, and includes (without in any way limiting thereto) all costs and cost escalations related to material, labor, transportation to the vessel, and testing, as well as Jamaican customs, duties, taxes, assessments, licenses and permits. The unit price of bauxite covered by this Agreement is firm and fixed and not subject to revision.

Part B: AGRICULTURAL COMMODITY PROVISIONS

Article VI: Contract Quantity

CCC agrees to sell, and BATCO agrees to purchase, 7,238 metric tons of nonfat dry milk (5,184 metric tons of medium heat and 2,054 metric tons of high heat) and 1,905 metric tons of anhydrous milkfat.

Article VII: Commodity Price

7.1 NONFAT DRY MILK

The price of the nonfat dry milk shall be U.S. $1,100 per metric ton, FAS Gulf ports, plus storage charges of U.S. $10 per metric ton for deliveries of nonfat dry milk made to Gulf ports after August 31, 1982. Delivery shall be evidenced by the date of the dock receipt.

7.2 ANHYDROUS MILKFAT

The price of the anhydrous milkfat shall be U.S. $2,625 per metric ton, FAS Gulf ports. No storage charges shall apply to deliveries of anhydrous milkfat.

Article VIII: Delivery Schedule

8.1 NONFAT DRY MILK

8.1.1 CCC shall deliver the nonfat dry milk to BATCO FAS Gulf ports in accordance with following schedule:

Delivery Month (1982)	*Medium Heat (MT)*	*High Heat (MT)*
May	594	250
June	650	100
July	650	284
August	650	284
September	650	284
October	650	284
November	670	284
December	670	284
TOTAL	5,184	2,054
GRAND TOTAL		7,238

8.1.2 In consideration of CCC's agreement to furnish nonfat dry milk manufactured within 90 calendar days from date of delivery to Gulf ports, CCC has the option to vary the quantities between medium heat and high heat nonfat dry milk each delivery month. However, CCC shall endeavor to deliver nonfat dry milk in accordance with the quantities of medium heat or high heat called for by the delivery schedule. CCC will adjust shipments in July, October and December so that the cumulative quantities of medium heat and high heat delivered will agree with the cumulative amounts called for by the delivery schedule.

8.2 ANHYDROUS MILKFAT

CCC shall deliver the anhydrous milkfat to BATCO FAS Gulf ports in accordance with the following delivery schedule:

Delivery Month	*Quantity (MT)*
July 1982	250
August	250
September	250
October	230
November	230
December	230
January 1983	230
February	235
TOTAL	1,905

8.3 NOTICE TO DELIVER

At least 21 days prior to the final date that CCC is to have the nonfat dry milk and anhydrous milkfat at port, BATCO shall furnish CCC with a notice to deliver listing the vessel name, estimated time of arrival and port, quantity of nonfat dry milk and anhydrous milkfat scheduled to be lifted, and stating whether the shipment is to be containerized or unitized, such as on pallets and stretch-wrapped. The notice shall be sent to the Kansas City Agricultural Stabilization and Conservation Service (ASCS) Commodity Office.

8.4 BATCO shall be responsible for all expenses after delivery by CCC of the nonfat dry milk and anhydrous milk to FAS Gulf port, including any expenses for failure of the vessel to lift all or part of the shipment as scheduled, pier or warehouse storage, rail, truck and/or barge demurrage, reinspection and deterioration. In the event CCC fails to deliver all or part of the quantity scheduled to be delivered each month, CCC shall be responsible for all expenses resulting from such failure including, but not limited to, dead freight and demurrage.

ARTICLE IX: QUALITY AND QUANTITY DETERMINATIONS

9.1 NONFAT DRY MILK

9.1.1 The nonfat dry milk shall be U.S. Extra Grade and shall meet the United States Standards for Grades of Nonfat Dry Milk (Spray Process), in effect on April 1, 1973, except that the moisture content must be no more than 3.7 percent. (Exhibit B-1)

9.1.2 The nonfat dry milk shall have been manufactured in the United States within 90 calendar days from date of delivery to Gulf ports. The date of delivery to port will be evidenced by the date of the dock receipt.

9.1.3 The nonfat dry milk shall be produced in a plant meeting the USDA requirements contained in the "General Specifications for Dairy Plants Approved for USDA Inspection and Grading Service." (Exhibit B-2)

9.1.4 Inspection and testing procedures for the nonfat dry milk to determine the grade and weight shall be in accordance with USDA General Instructions for Sampling NDM dated July 13, 1970, as revised (DA INST. NO. 918-30) and USDA Methods of Laboratory Analysis for Nonfat Dry Milk dated November 30, 1972 (DA INST. NO. 918-103-1) (Exhibit B-3).

9.1.5 BATCO shall have the right of reinspection of the nonfat dry milk at the U.S. port of export and the right to reject any nonfat dry milk which does not meet the terms and conditions of this Agreement.

9.2 ANHYDROUS MILKFAT

9.2.1 The anhydrous milkfat shall have a flavor similar to bland, unmelted, unsalted, uncultured, fresh cream butter; when heated to approximately 140 F, be clear; and have a uniform light yellow to golden color. It shall be free from objectionable foreign flavors and odors, such as rancid, scorched, stale, oxidized or metallic. The anhydrous milkfat shall be free from lumps or large crystals, be smooth with the interior free of air bubbles and contain no antioxidants.

In addition, the anhydrous milkfat shall meet the following analytical requirements:

(a) Milkfat—not less than 99.8 percent

(b) Moisture—not more than 0.15 percent

(c) Free fatty acids—not more than 0.3 percent (calculated as oleic acid)

(d) Peroxide value—not more than 0.1 milligram equivalent per kilogram of fat

9.2.2 The product shall be produced in a plant meeting the USDA requirements contained in the "General Specifications for Dairy Plants Approved for USDA Inspection and Grading Service". (Exhibit B-2)

9.2.3 Inspection and testing procedures for the purpose of determining the quality of the anhydrous milkfat shall be in accordance with USDA Methods of Laboratory Analysis for Moisture, Fat, Salt, Curd and PH dated November 30, 1972 (DA INST. NO. 918-101-1). (Exhibit B-4)

9.2.4 The anhydrous milkfat must meet the required specifications and standards published in the Federal Register, Vol. 40 No. 198 of October 10, 1975. (Exhibit B-2)

9.2.5 BATCO shall have the right of reinspection of the anhydrous milkfat at the U.S. port of export and the right to reject any anhydrous milkfat which does not meet the terms and conditions of this Agreement.

ARTICLE X: PACKAGING AND MARKING

10.1 NONFAT DRY MILK

10.1.1 *Packaging Description:* The nonfat dry milk will be packed in 50 pound (22.68 kilos) sacks constructed of 3 layer kraft paper and a loose-inserted 4 mil-low density food grade polyethylene liner. Sacks may be sealed by sewing horizontally along the upper edge without sewing the polyethylene liner, or the sacks may be sealed with heat. If bags are sewn, exposed threads will be covered with paper to prevent insect and dust penetration into the powder. The loose-inserted polyethylene liner will be gathered in the form of a goose neck and tied.

10.1.2 *Packaging and Markings:* Sacks containing the nonfat dry milk shall be marked to show the following:

(a) Name of product.

(b) Name and location of manufacturing plant or plant number.

(c) Month and year manufactured.

(d) Manufacturer's lot number.

(e) Marked net weight of 50 lbs.

(f) The sacks containing high heat nonfat dry milk will have a clearly visible red marking on the outer layer of each sack. The medium heat nonfat dry milk will not have these special distinctive markings.

10.2 ANHYDROUS MILKFAT

10.2.1 *Container Description:* The anhydrous milkfat shall be packed in new 55 gallon nonreturnable steel drums. The drums shall be

Type II, liquid tight, 18 gage or heavier closed-head cylindrical steel, with double seamed chimes, flat heads, integral chime reinforcement, expanded side wall consisting of a series of parallel circumferential beads meeting the requirements of Federal Specification PPP-D-1152 or PPP-D-729 (Exhibit B-5). Steel cap seals shall be applied to each closure in accordance with PPP-D-729 or PPP-D-1152 (Exhibit B-5). The drums shall be lined with a Food and Drug Administration approved food-grade liner recommended for contact with anhydrous milkfat. The drums shall contain anhydrous milkfat weighing approximately 440 pounds net (200 kilos). The drums will be vacuum sealed, or a nitrogen blanket may be applied to eliminate air in the drum. The drums containing anhydrous milkfat will be transported to Gulf ports and stored at port without refrigeration.

10.2.2 *Labeling and Marking:* The following information shall be indicated on the exterior of the drum:
(a) Name of product
(b) Date of manufacture (day, month, year)
(c) "Keep Refrigerated"—(32 F to 40 F)

ARTICLE XI: DOCUMENTS REQUIRED

11.1 NONFAT DRY MILK

11.1.1 CCC shall furnish to BATCO an inspection and grading certificate issued by the U.S. Department of Agriculture showing the manufacture date, weight, quality and origin of the nonfat dry milk. The inspection and grading certificate will show the nonfat dry milk to be extra grade, to have been manufactured in the United States within 90 calendar days from the date of delivery to Gulf ports, and that the moisture content is no more than 3.7 percent. The inspection and grading certificate will be the only document required to be presented by CCC evidencing the quality, weight, origin and date of manufacture of the nonfat dry milk.

11.1.2 CCC will furnish to BATCO a copy of (a) any over, short or damage report for each shipment; (b) a dock receipt; and (c) a consignee receipt.

11.1.3 BATCO will furnish to CCC one copy of the signed on-board ocean bill of lading showing the ultimate destination of the nonfat dry milk as Jamaica.

11.2 ANHYDROUS MILKFAT

11.2.1 CCC shall furnish to BATCO an inspection and grading certificate issued by the U.S. Department of Agriculture showing the laboratory analysis, manufacture date, weight, the place of manufacture of the anhydrous milkfat and a health statement that reads—"The anhydrous milkfat was manufactured in a plant inspected and approved by the U.S. Department of Agriculture as operating under sanitary conditions and the anhydrous milkfat was considered suitable for human consumption at the time of inspection and laboratory analysis." The inspector and grading certificate will show that the anhydrous milkfat was manufactured in the United States and meets the specifications required by this Agreement. The inspection and grading certificate will be the only document required to be presented by CCC evidencing the quality, weight and origin of the anhydrous milkfat.

11.2.2 CCC will furnish to BATCO a copy of (a) any over, short or damage report for each shipment; (b) a dock receipt; and (c) a consignee receipt.

11.2.3 BATCO will furnish to CCC one copy of the signed on-board ocean bill of lading showing the ultimate destination of the anhydrous milkfat as Jamaica.

11.3 TRANSMITTAL OF DOCUMENTS

CCC shall furnish BATCO, or its designated agent, with an invoice and a copy of each required document promptly after each shipment. BATCO shall notify the Kansas City ASCS Commodity Office of its designated agent to which the documents are to be sent promptly after the signing of this Agreement.

ARTICLE XII: PAYMENT FOR THE AGRICULTURAL COMMODITIES

12.1 Payment to CCC for the FAS value of the nonfat dry milk and anhydrous milkfat delivered to and accepted by BATCO shall be paid for by BATCO by delivery to CCC, in accordance with Part A of this Agreement, of a quantity of bauxite equivalent in total value to the total FAS value of the nonfat dry milk and anhydrous milkfat delivered. CCC will establish a "barter account" in which the value of exports of nonfat dry milk and anhydrous milkfat will be applied against the value of the bauxite delivered to CCC in accordance with Part A of this Agreement.

12.2 If the total value of the nonfat dry milk and anhydrous milkfat delivered to BATCO exceeds the value of the bauxite received by CCC, BATCO shall make payment to CCC for such excess value in U.S. dollars.

12.3 If the value of the bauxite delivered to CCC exceeds the total value of the nonfat dry milk and anhydrous milkfat delivered to BATCO, CCC shall make payment to BATCO for such excess in U.S. dollars.

ARTICLE XIII: EXPORT REQUIREMENTS

13.1 BATCO shall export the nonfat dry milk and anhydrous milk delivered by CCC only to Jamaica. The nonfat dry milk and anhydrous milk shall not be reentered by anyone into the United States nor shall BATCO cause the nonfat dry milk and anhydrous milkfat to be transshipped to any other country.

13.2 The sale by CCC of the nonfat dry milk and anhydrous milkfat covered by this Agreement is made upon condition that BATCO complies with the export requirements of this Agreement. If the nonfat dry milk and anhydrous milkfat delivered by CCC is not exported or is reentered into the United States, the purchase price with respect to the quantity of nonfat dry milk involved shall be adjusted upward to the domestic unrestricted use price of $2,280 per metric ton and the contract price with respect to the quantity of anhydrous milkfat involved shall be adjusted upward to the domestic unrestricted use price for U.S. extra grade butter of $3,686 per metric ton, plus $988 per metric ton which reflects generally the processing charges paid by CCC to convert cream to anhydrous milkfat plus the cost of the drums in which the anhydrous milkfat is packed and the estimated shrinkage which occurs in processing cream into anhydrous milkfat.

13.3 The total amount of upward adjustment in the purchase price shall be paid by BATCO in U.S. dollars to CCC promptly on demand, plus interest on the upward adjustment in the purchase price at the rate of nineteen (19) percent per annum from the date of signing this Agreement.

13.4 An upward adjustment of the purchase price for nonfat dry milk and anhydrous milkfat not exported, or which is reentered into the United States, will not be made if CCC determines that:

(a) The nonfat dry milk or anhydrous milkfat purchased from CCC was lost, damaged, destroyed, or deteriorated and the physical condition thereof was such that its entry into domestic market channels will not impair CCC's price support operations: *Provided,* that if insurance proceeds or other recoveries (such as from carriers) exceed the purchase price of the nonfat dry milk or anhydrous milkfat lost, damaged, destroyed, or deteriorated, plus other costs incurred by BATCO in connection with such nonfat dry milk or anhydrous milkfat prior to the time of its loss, the amount of such excess shall be paid to CCC; or

(b) The nonfat dry milk or anhydrous milkfat was reentered into the United States without the fault or negligence of BATCO and was subsequently exported in accordance with the provisions of this Agreement.

13.5 If any quantity of nonfat dry milk or anhydrous milkfat is transshipped, or caused to be transshipped by BATCO to any country other than Jamaica, BATCO shall be in default and shall be subject to the applicable upward purchase price adjustment specified in Paragraph 13.2 of this Article XIII.

PART C: GENERAL PROVISIONS

ARTICLE XIV: MANAGEMENT COMMITTEE

14.1 COMMITTEE

Promptly after the signing of this Agreement, the parties hereto shall establish a Management Committee to oversee the performance of this Agreement. CCC shall appoint to be members of such committee an individual in the Department of Agriculture to represent its interests with respect to terms of this Agreement covering the anhydrous milkfat and nonfat dry milk and an individual in the General Services Administration to represent its interests with respect to the terms of this Agreement covering the bauxite. BATCO shall appoint two individuals to be a member of such committee. Each party shall also appoint an alternate member(s). The Management Committee will not be empowered to revise or amend this Agreement.

14.2 COORDINATION

Subject to requirements set forth in this Agreement, the Management Committee will coordinate efforts among the parties and resolve problems which may arise in the administration of this Agreement. Meetings may be called by either party upon seven days notice and will be held at the principal location of the non-requesting party. An agenda will be proposed for each meeting and distributed by the host at least three working days prior to the meeting. Minutes of each meeting will be published by the host within five working days after the meeting.

14.3 DELEGATION OF AUTHORITY

14.3.1 CCC reserves the right to delegate to the GSA any and all authority to act as its agent in carrying out the terms and conditions of Part A of this Agreement as they relate to the shipment, handling and storing of the bauxite.

14.3.2 BATCO reserves the right to delegate to Jamaica Commodity Trading Company, Ltd. any and all authority to act as its agent in carrying out the terms and conditions of Part B of this Agreement as they relate to the shipment of the agricultural commodities.

ARTICLE XV: DISPUTES

Any dispute arising under PART B of this Agreement concerning a question of fact or law which is not disposed of by mutual agreement between the parties hereto, shall be finally settled under the Rules of Conciliation and Arbitration of the International Chamber of Commerce by one or more arbitrators appointed in accordance with the rules thereof. The Agreement will be governed by the laws of the State of New York.

ARTICLE XVI: NOTICES

All notices required or permitted to be given under this Agreement shall be given in writing and by registered air mail or cable addressed to such party at the following addresses:

16.1 PART A—BAUXITE PROVISIONS

Jamaica Government
c/o The Bauxite and Alumina
Trading Company, Limited
5th Floor, 63 Knutsford
Boulevard
Kingston, 5, Jamaica, W.I.
Telex: 2467, JABM JA

General Services Administration
Agent for Commodity Credit
Corporation
18th & F. Streets, NW

Federal Property Resources
Service—D
Washington, DC 20405
Telex No. 89.2515

16.2 PART B—AGRICULTURAL COMMODITY PROVISIONS

Commodity Credit Corporation
14th Street and Independence
Avenue, SW
Washington, D.C. 20250
Telex: 8-9491
Telephone: (202) 382-9254 or
447-6301

Jamaica Government
c/o The Bauxite and Alumina
Trading Company, Limited
(BATCO)
5th Floor, 63 Knutsford
Boulevard
Kingston, 5, Jamaica, W.I.
Telex: 2467, JABM JA

Kansas City Agricultural
Stabilization and Conservation
Service (ASCS) Commodity
Office
P.O. Box 8510
Kansas City, Missouri 64114
Telex: 434126
Telephone: (816) 976-6140

ARTICLE XVII: FORCE MAJEURE

Neither BATCO nor CCC shall be liable for any failure or delay in complying with their respective responsibilities under this Agreement caused in whole or in part by force majeure which shall include, but not be restricted to, acts of God or of the public enemy, acts of the Government, fires, floods, epidemics, quarantine, restrictions, strikes, freight embargoes, and unusually severe weather; however, in every case, the failure to perform must be beyond the control and without the fault or negligence of the party to the Agreement seeking excuse from liability.

ARTICLE XVIII: OTHER PROVISIONS (PART A ONLY)

18.1 APPLICABLE TO ENTIRE PART A

The following clauses apply to Part A of this Agreement. Wherever the word "contract" appears, it shall be deemed to mean this Agreement. Wherever the word "contractor" appears, it shall be deemed to mean "BATCO".

(i) Definitions, Clause 1, Standard Form 32 (copy attached)
(ii) Assignment of Claims, Clause 8, Standard Form 32 (copy attached)
(iii) Examination of Records by Comptroller General, Clause 10, Standard Form 32 (copy attached)

(iv) Disputes Clause, Clause 12, Standard Form (copy attached)
(v) Use of U.S. Flag Commercial Vessels, Clause 57, GSA Form 1424 (copy attached)
(vi) Pricing of Adjustments, Clause 24, Standard Form 32 (copy attached)

18.2 APPLICABLE TO WORK PERFORMED IN THE U.S. UNDER PART A

BATCO shall include the following clauses in any subcontract work to be performed in the United States:

(i) Clauses from Standard Form 32 (copy attached):
15. Convict Labor
16. Contract Work Hours and Safety Standard Act-Overtime Compensation
18. Equal Opportunity

(ii) Clauses from GSA Form 1424 (copy attached):
59. Clean Air and Water
62. Disabled Veteran and Veterans of the Vietnam Era
65. Cost or Pricing Data Requirements

(iii) Clauses (attached):
Small Business and Small Disadvantaged Business Subcontracting Labor
Surplus Area Subcontracting Program
Women Owned Business Concerns Subcontracting Program

ARTICLE XIX: AMENDMENTS

Any amendments to this Agreement must be in writing and require the signature of both parties in order to be valid. Such amendments shall be expressly designated as amendments hereto and numbered consecutively.

ARTICLE XX: DURATION

This Agreement shall remain in effect for the period starting with the signature of both parties until the mutual obligations herein have been completed.

In witness whereof, this Agreement has been executed by and on behalf of CCC and BATCO by their respective duly authorized officers.

FOR THE GOVERNMENT OF THE UNITED STATES

FOR THE GOVERNMENT OF JAMAICA

BY ______________________________ BY ___________________________

General Sales Manager and Vice
President, Commodity
Credit Corporation

Date 25 February, 1982

appendix

C

Western Chemical Compensation Agreements with Eastern Europe and the Soviet Union*

*From Ronald J. deMarinis et al., *Analysis of Recent Trends in U.S. Countertrade*, USITC Publication 1237, March 1982, p. 44.

Western Company	Year Contract Signed	Eastern Country	Equipment Supplied	Total Value of Eastern Export (in million $)	Planned Yearly Value of Exports (in million $)	Time Span of Buyback Deliveries
Occidental Petroleum (U.S.)	1978	Poland	Phosphate rock	670	33.5	1978–1997
Rhone Poulenc/Institute Francais du Petrole (France)	1975	Poland	Chemicals and textile fibers	NA	NA	NA
Ugine Kuhlmann (France)	1976	Poland	Unspecified cooperation in chemical production	NA	NA	NA
Uhde/Hoechst (West Germany)	1976	East Germany	Complex of 4 plants including 1 for producing caustic soda	32	4	1980–1987
Catalytic (United Kingdom)	1977	East Germany	Chlorine plant	11.5	2.3	NA
Petrocarbon Developments (United Kingdom)	1975	Poland	Chlorine plant (part of larger deal)	NA	NA	1980–1989
Krebs/Klockner (France and West Germany)	1975	Poland	Soda ash plant	180	30	1980–1985
De Nora (Italy)	1978	Romania	2 chlorine plants	NA	NA	NA
Chemie Linz (Austria)	1976	East Germany	Pesticides, herbicide agents and fertilizers	58.58	NA	NA
Vereinigte Edelstahlwerke (Austria)	1977	East Germany	Fine steel products	NA	NA	NA
Haldor Topsoe (Denmark)	1978	Bulgaria	Ammonia plant	7	1	1978–1984

Creusot Loire (France)	1976	Poland	2 ammonia plants	520	52	1983–1992
Creusot Loire (France)	1974	U.S.S.R.	4 ammonia plants	270	27	1980–1989
Occidental Petroleum (U.S.)	1974	U.S.S.R.	Building facilities for storing and handling fertilizers, including ammonia and deliveries of superphosphoric acid	10,000	441	1978–1997
Klockner/Davy Powergas (West Germany and United Kingdom)	1977	U.S.S.R.	Phthalic anhydride plant and maleic anhydride plant	20	2	1980–1989
Snamprogetti/Anic (Italy)	1975	U.S.S.R.	3 urea plants	115	11.5	1979–1988
Montedison (Italy)	1973	U.S.S.R.	3 urea plants	287	28.7 (ammonia)	1978–1987
				78	7.8 (urea)	1976–1985
Mitsui/Toyo (Japan)	1976	U.S.S.R.	4 ammonia plants	240	11	1977–1997
Klockner/Davy Powergas (West Germany and United Kingdom)	1976	U.S.S.R.	Phthalic anhydride plant, fumaric acid unit	20	2	1980–1989
Krupp led consortium (West Germany)	1976	Poland	Coal gasification plants	NA	NA	NA
ENI (Italy)	1975	U.S.S.R.	2 urea plants	NA	NA	NA
Lurgi (West Germany)	1976	Bulgaria	Polypropylene plant	NA	NA	NA
Mitsui (Japan)		East Germany	Benzene plant (part of aromatics complex)	150	25	1983–1988
Technip (France)	1976	U.S.S.R.	2 aromatics complexes	950	95	1980–1989

NA = not available.

Western Company	Year Contract Signed	Eastern Country	Equipment Supplied	Total Value of Eastern Export (in million $)	Planned Yearly Value of Exports (in million $)	Time Span of Buyback Deliveries
Krupp/Koppers (West Germany)	1976	U.S.S.R.	Dimethylterephthalate plant	100	10	1981–1990
Uhde/Hoechst (West Germany)	1977	U.S.S.R.	Polyester staple fiber plant	NA	9	1981–1987
Rhone-Poulenc (France)	1976	U.S.S.R.	Complex deal including supply of equipment and chemicals	NA	NA	1984–1993
Chisso (Japan)	1972	Czechoslovakia	Polypropylene plant	NA	5	NA
Salzgitter (West Germany)	1972	U.S.S.R.	Polyethylene plant	170	13	1971–1983
Salzgitter (West Germany)	1973	U.S.S.R.	Polyethylene plant	225	25	1978–1986
CJB/Union Carbide (United Kingdom and U.S.)	1974	U.S.S.R.	Polyethylene plant	70	7	1980–1989
CJB/Union Carbide (United Kingdom and U.S.)	1977	U.S.S.R.	Polyethylene plant	162	16	1933–1993
Litwin (France)	1973	U.S.S.R.	Plants to produce styrene and polystyrene.	160	19	1979–1987
Marubeni (Japan)	1975	U.S.S.R.	Expansion of plant to 75,000 t/yr of acrylonitrile	30	6	1978–1982
Montedison (Italy)	1973	U.S.S.R.	Acrylonitrile plant	150	15	1980–1990
Krupp/Koppers (West Germany)	1976	U.S.S.R.	DMT plant	100	10	1981–1990

Krupp/Koppers (West Germany)	1978	U.S.S.R.	DMT plant	150	15	1981–1990
Uhde/Hoechst (West Germany)	1977	U.S.S.R.	Polyester staple fiber plant	NA	9	1981–1990
Technip/Technipetrol (France and Italy)	1972	Bulgaria	Ethylene plant	10	2.2	1979–1983
Salzgitter (West Germany)	1976	U.S.S.R.	Ethylene oxide plant	100	10	1979–1988
Lummus/Monsanto (U.S.)	1975	U.S.S.R.	Acetic acid plant	NA	NA	NA
Snia Viscosa (Italy)	1975	U.S.S.R.	Caprolactam plant	224	28	NA
Klockner/Davy Powergas (West Germany and United Kingdom)	1976	U.S.S.R.	Phthalic anhydride plant and fumaric acid unit	50	7	1980–1989
Klockner/Davy Powergas (West Germany and United Kingdom)	1977	U.S.S.R.	Phthalic anhydride plant and maleic anhydride plant	50	7	1980–1989
Hoechst/Uhde/Wacker (West Germany)	1974	U.S.S.R.	VCM plant	66	16.5	1976–1979
Klockner/Hols (West Germany)	1974	U.S.S.R.	PVC plant	33	3.30	NA
Klockner/Hols (West Germany)	1974	Bulgaria	PVC plant	25	3.5	1980–1988
Klockner/Hols (West Germany)	1974	U.S.S.R.	PVC plant	54	5.4	1978–1987
Uhde/Hoechst (West Germany)	1976	East Germany	PVC plant	80	10	1980–1987
Kommerling (West Germany)	1977	Hungary	License and equipment for making windows from synthetic materials	NA	NA	NA

NA = not available.

Western Company	Year Contract Signed	Eastern Country	Equipment Supplied	Total Value of Eastern Export (in million $)	Planned Yearly Value of Exports (in million $)	Time Span of Buyback Deliveries
Chemie Linz/Voest Alpine (Austria)	1974	Poland	Melamine resin plant	NA	NA	NA
Dow Chemical Europe (West Germany)	1977	East Germany	Propylene oxide	85	NA	1979–1988
Montedison (Italy)	1973	U.S.S.R.	11 chemical plants	57.5	5.75	1980–1990
Rhone-Poulenc (France)	1976	U.S.S.R.	Complex deals including supply of equipments and chemicals	34.5	3.45	1981–1990
Krupp/Koppers (Germany)	1976	U.S.S.R.	Dimethylterephthalate plant	100	10	1981–1990
Davy Powergas/ICI/Klockner (United Kingdom and West Germany)	1977	U.S.S.R.	2 methanol plants	345	34.5	1981–1990
Uhde-Hoechst (West Germany)	1977	U.S.S.R.	Polyester staple fiber plant	NA	9	1981–1987

NA = not available.

Source: Compiled by U.S. International Trade Commission from various published sources including "Soviet Chemical Equipment Purchases from the West: Impact on Production and Foreign Trade," Central Intelligence Agency, October 1978, and "East-West Trade in Chemicals," Organization for Economic Cooperation and Development, 1980.

appendix

D

Compensation Frame Contracts*

*From Pompiliu Verzariu, *Countertrade Practices in East Europe, the Soviet Union and China: An Introductory Guide to Business*, U.S. Department of Commerce, International Trade Administration, April 1980, p. 70.

Draft of an Indirect Compensation Contract with Romania

FRAME CONTRACT

concluded on the .... between .... and ROMCHIM, Bucharest, Bd. Dacia 13.

CHAPTER I

1. ROMCHIM and Messrs. .... have concluded the contract Nr. .... for the supply of .... amounting to ....
2. Further to the above conclusion, Messrs. .... oblige themselves to purchase Romanian commodities mutually agreed upon, directly or through third firms, under competitive conditions to be established from case to case.
3. The value of Romanian commodities agreed upon represents ....% of the contract value, that is .... out of which
4. Messrs. .... oblige themselves to buy and pay the Romanian goods foreseen under Point 3 above before ....

CHAPTER II—GUARANTEE

In case of failure of Messrs. .... to fulfill their obligations in contractual time, or if they fulfill them only partially, the company shall pay to ROMCHIM a penalty of ....% on the nonfulfilled partial value of the obligation. As a guarantee of the penalty payment Messrs. .... will remit in favour of ROMCHIM bank letter of guarantee (according to the attached draft) issued by a corresponding bank of the Romanian Bank for Foreign Trade.

The receipt of the aforementioned bank guarantee letter conditions the acknowledgement on the part of Messrs. ROMCHIM of entering into force of the contract Nr. ....

CHAPTER III—ARBITRATION—Art. .... of the contract Nr. ....

CHAPTER IV—FINAL PROVISIONS

The contractual parties agree upon that only those export contracts concluded with the Romanian exporting enterprises can be taken into consideration, as countertrade, which stipulate precisely a clause that "the export contract constitutes a countertrade to contract Nr. . . . ."

Only the values of the goods contracted, delivered and payed after the coming into force of the contract Nr. . . . . will be deducted.

The values deducted are only the FOB and/or franco border of the exporting country values.

Irrespective of their value, or object, no contracts will be entered into without reference to the clauses in this contract.

Messrs. . . . . and ROMCHIM shall keep record of the export operations contracted according to this Frame Contract.

The parties shall quarterly compare their records.

This Frame Contract is an integral part of contract Nr. . . . . and enters into force at the same time as the contract Nr. . . . .

ROMCHIM
Bucharest

BANK LETTER OF GUARANTEE

for the fulfillment of contract Nr. . . . . of . . . .
ROMANIAN BANK FOR FOREIGN TRADE
Bucharest

Messrs. ROMCHIM, Bucharest, and Messrs. . . . . have concluded on the . . . . the Frame Contract Nr. . . . . through which Messrs. . . . . obliged themselves to buy Romanian commodities according to Chap. I, Art. 3 and 4 and to Chap. IV, Par. 1 and 2 as follows:

Chap. I—Art. 3 ". . . . ."
—Art. 4 ". . . . ."
Chap. IV (par. 1 and 2)
". . . . ."
". . . . ."

In case of nonfulfillment of the obligations stipulated in the Frame Contract Nr. . . . . according to Chap. II of the aforementioned Frame Contract, Messrs. . . . . are obligated to pay a penalty guaranteed by a bank letter of guarantee, that is: Chap. II ". . . . ."

According to the stipulations above, we oblige ourselves irrevocably to pay in favor of Messrs. ROMCHIM up to the amount of . . . . any sum requested by you invoking Chap. II reproduced above, at your first and simple demand without any other proof except your declaration that Messrs.

. . . . have not complied with obligations foreseen in Chap. II of the Frame Contract Nr. . . . . concluded with Messrs. ROMCHIM.

By virtue of this letter of guarantee we will immediately effect the payments, deliberately renouncing the benefit of discussions, without having the right on our part of opposing the payments requested, or to invoke another objection or any other formality of any kind on the part of Messrs. . . . . or on our part, nor to invoke currency restrictions on which Messrs. . . . . could prevail, and without being necessary for you to have recourse against Messrs. . . . ., or to Arbitration or to any Tribunal.

The validity of this letter of guarantee expires 30 days after the time limit foreseen in Chap. I Art. 4 of the Frame Contract Nr. . . . . for purchasing the Romanian commodities, but can be automatically extended, without any formality with the delays agreed by the partners of the abovementioned Frame Contract.

After the obligation under this letter of guarantee has been performed, this letter of guarantee shall be returned to us.

____
(Bank)

Draft of an Indirect Compensation Agreement with the U.S.S.R.

FRAME CONTRACT

1. In connection with the signing of the present Contract the parties have agreed that the Sellers will purchase from Soviet Foreign Trade organizations within the period of . . . . machines and/or equipment in the amount of . . . . it being understood that the prices for the above machines and/or equipment will be of the world level.

2. The quantity and detailed specification of the machines and/or equipment as well as the prices, time and other conditions of the delivery must be agreed upon between the Sellers and the corresponding Soviet Foreign Trade organization not later than . . . . from the date of signing the present Contract.

3. The Sellers will immediately notify the Buyers that the transaction has been concluded by sending to them a copy of the Contract concluded with the Soviet Foreign Trade organization. In the Contract there should be reference to the present Contract.

4. In case of nonfulfillment by the Sellers of the above obligation, the Buyers have the right to deduct the sum, stated in Clause 1 of the present Article, from the Sellers' invoices. Should for any reason the stated sum not be deducted by the Buyers while paying the Sellers' invoices, the latter are to pay this sum at the first demand of the Buyers.

deducted by the Buyers while paying the Sellers' invoices, the latter are to pay this sum at the first demand of the Buyers.

Draft of a Direct Compensation Contract with the People's Republic of China

PRODUCTION CONTRACT

1. Sellers undertake to produce .... (product for Buyers) with material from Buyers on processing fees basis. Designs, specifications, quantity and rate or processing fees for such production will be stipulated in separate contracts as agreed upon by both parties.
2. Buyers undertake to provide Sellers with required processing equipment and equipment for production and maintenance of toolings for a total value of HK$ .... as per Appendix I attached.
3. To compensate the cost of equipment provided by Buyers, a special discount of .... percent of invoice value will be deducted from the processing fees. Such deduction will be effected from the first shipment of goods supplied by Sellers until the total value of equipment is fully reimbursed. Materials and dies are to be supplied by Buyers free of charge to Sellers.
4. All equipment to be provided by Buyers will be delivered in one or more shipments to arrive Shanghai latest by the end of 1978. Buyers will send technical staff to Shanghai to assist in installation and to render technical advice. Adequate quantity of materials, corresponding to the quantity of contracted production under this agreement with reasonable allowance of waste is to be delivered by Buyers to Sellers. First shipment of material should be delivered within 30 days after arrival of the equipment at Shanghai.
5. It is mutually agreed that the first lot of products to be processed will not be less than .... (quantity) pieces each of Buyers' design No. .... Specifications and quality of products will conform to Buyers' samples submitted. (Four sealed samples each are in possession of Buyers and Sellers for reference.) Finished products will be delivered to Buyers within 60 days after arrival of the materials at Shanghai.
6. Sellers hereby indemnify Buyers from any loss or damage caused by de-

viation of quality or specification. Discrepancies resulted by contingencies beyond human control will be settled by means of mutual negotiation.

7. Sellers' agree not to sell or supply any products under Buyers' design to any parties other than the Buyers.
8. This agreement will have effect from .... (date) for .... years and the duration may be extended or amended by negotiation.

Letter Of Undertaking with Indonesia*

Department of Trade and Cooperatives
Republic of Indonesia
Directorat General for Foreign Trade
Jalan Abdul Muis 87
Jakarta
INDONESIA

c/o (Insert name of Department, Agency or
Corporation issuing tender document)

Dear Sirs:

We refer to (describe subject matter of tender) and to our tender document no. .... submitted on .... 19 ... . pursuant to tender document no. .... issued by (insert name of Indonesian Department, Agency or Corporation issuing tender document).

If we are selected as (contractor) (supplier) in respect of the above-described tender, we hereby irrevocably undertake during the period from the date of award of the contract relating to such tender until final acceptance (or equivalent) of our work and services thereunder:

1. To purchase, or to cause to be purchased by one or more of our affiliated companies in (insert name of country and nationality of contractor/supplier) or by third parties located in such country acceptable to you, agricultural and/or industrial products contained in the most recent "List of Indonesian Export Commodities Available for Additional Exports" published by the Department of Trade and Cooperatives (hereinafter the "Products") from one or more of the commodity associations or exporters named in the "List of Indonesian Commodity Associations and Exporters" published by the Department of Trade and Cooperatives (hereinafter

*Source: Department of Trade and Cooperatives, Republic of Indonesia.

the "Exporters") in an amount at least equal to the foreign currency value of all equipment and materials to be supplied by us from non-Indonesian sources pursuant to the terms of the above-described contract;

2. To use the Products, or to resell the Products for use, or to cause the Products to be used or resold, in (insert name of country and nationality of contractor/supplier), unless with your specific authorization we are permitted to use the Products, or to resell the Products for use, or to cause the Products to be used or resold, in any other country;
3. To purchase the Products, or to cause the Products to be purchased, periodically over the term of the contract relating to the above-described tender in such a manner as to avoid the situation arising where the Products to be acquired pursuant to this undertaking must be purchased at the end of the term of such contract; and
4. To submit, or to cause to be submitted, to the Department of Trade and Cooperatives copies of all contracts with and purchase orders issued to Exporters relating to the purchase of Products pursuant to this undertaking, and to cause each such contract and purchase order relating to the purchase of Products by any third party as aforesaid to refer specifically to this undertaking, in each case to permit the Department of Trade and Cooperatives to monitor compliance herewith.

In connection with our irrevocable undertaking contained herein, this will confirm our understanding that:

a. The commercial terms, including those relating to price and delivery, in respect of each purchase of Products from an Exporter shall be negotiated by us or by other purchasers thereof at the time of actual purchase;
b. The amount of each such purchase to be applied towards our obligation hereunder shall be equal to the invoiced purchase price of the Products purchased, excluding, however, any shipping costs included in such invoice and any taxes or customs duties charged in connection therewith;
c. The amount of each such purchase (if measured in a currency other than the currency in which our obligation hereunder is measured) shall be applied against our obligation hereunder at exchange rates (as quoted by Bank Indonesia) prevailing at the date of the Exporter's invoice issued in respect of such purchase; and
d. Our undertaking contained herein shall be in addition to, and not by way of credit against, any commitments or other arrangements in effect on the date hereof with respect to the purchase of Products by purchasers located in (insert name of country of contractor/supplier).

If we fail to comply with our undertaking contained herein, we hereby agree to pay to you as liquidated damages an amount equal to 50% of the difference between the total value of products actually purchased pursuant to this undertaking and the total foreign currency value of all equipment and materials actually supplied by us from non-Indonesian sources pursuant to the terms of the contract awarded in respect of the above-described tender.

In connection with our undertaking contained herein, we hereby represent and warrant to you that (i) we have full power and authority and legal right to enter into this undertaking and to perform and observe the terms and provisions hereof, (ii) we have taken all necessary legal action to authorize, execute and deliver this undertaking, (iii) this undertaking constitutes our legal, valid and binding obligation, and (iv) no law, rule or regulation of contractual or other obligation binding on us is or will be contravened by reason of our execution and delivery of this undertaking or by our performance and observance of the terms and provisions hereof.

This undertaking shall be binding upon our successors.

This undertaking has been executed on our behalf by our duly authorized Indonesian commercial representative/agent and such execution shall be deemed to bind us in all respects as regards the subject matter hereof. We hereby agree to countersign this undertaking if so requsted by you.

Very truly yours,

(NAME OF TENDERER)
By
Name
Title

ADDITIONAL PARAGRAPH TO LETTER OF UNDERTAKING

(I) If during the course of performance of our obligation contained herein, we should be of the view that sufficient products either are not available in Indonesia or are not of suitable export quality or internationally competitive in price, you shall, at your request, review with us the actual circumstances at the time and

(II) If, after both parties have reviewed the matter in good faith and in the spirit of cooperation, we mutually agree that we are not able to comply with the requirements of our undertaking contained herein because sufficient products either are not available in Indonesia or are not of suitable export quality or internationally competitive in price, or available for certain destinations,

You shall in good faith modify such requirements to take account of actual circumstances at the time which modifications will include, without limitation, an extension of the time which our obligations contained herein must be satisfied.

We further mutually agree that the review and modification(s) will be conducted with a view toward reaching a mutually acceptable solution and the avoidance of a dispute.

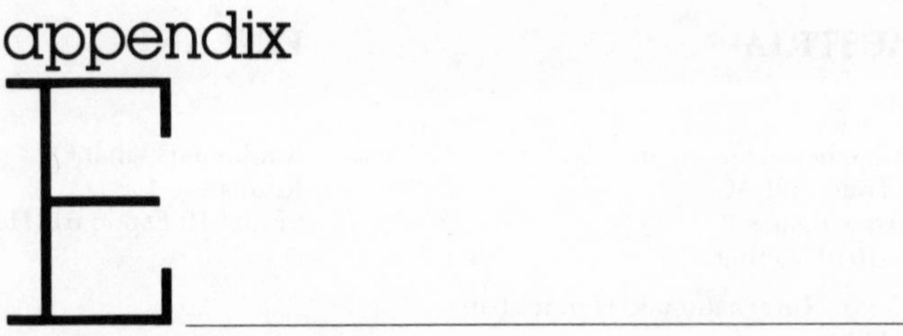

appendix E

International Trading Houses*

*This is a partial list of the many firms that engage in trading and occasional countertrading. The list should be regarded as a guide only and does not pretend to be comprehensive or have any endorsement. In addition to the firms listed, several financial institutions in western Europe and the United States also provide services related to countertrade.

AUSTRIA

Allgemeine Finanz-und-Waren-Treuhand AG.
Strauchgasse 3
A-1010 Vienna

Centro Internationale Handelsbank AG.
Bauernmarkt 6
A-1010 Vienna

Centropa Handelsgesellschaft mbH.
Selerstatte 15
A-1010 Vienna

Evidenzburo für Aussenhandelsgeschafte (EFAG)
Brucknerstrasse 4
A-1040 Vienna

Gebruder Schoeller OHG.
Renngasse 1
A-1011 Vienna

Voest Alpine Intertrading GmbH.
Schmiedegasse 14
A-4041 Linz

BELGIUM

Belgafric
142A Avenue Louise
B-1170 Brussels

Devetra Trade Development Corporation
Chaussee de Charleroi 54
B-1060 Brussels

Interocean SA.
Chaussee de la Hulpe 181, Bte. 5
B-1170 Brussels

DENMARK

Interkompens
Studiesstraede 63
Copenhagen V

FINLAND

Kaukomarkkinat OY
Kutojantie 4
SF-02610 Espoo 61, Helsinki

FRANCE

Lafitte International
Rue Lafitte 21
F-75009 Paris

Louis Dreyfus & Co.
6 Rue Rabelais
Paris 8e

J.A. Goldschmidt SA.
149 Rue Honore
Paris 1er

Graficomex
20 Rue de la Ville L'Eveque
F-75008 Paris

Secopa
22 Rue d'Aguesseau
F-75008 Paris

ITALY

Compagnia Generale Interscambi SpA. (COGIS)
Corso Venezia 54
I-20121 Milan

Novasider SpA.
Via San Francesco da Paola 17
I-10123 Torino

Sirco Trading SpA.
Via Serra 4
I-1621 Genoa

Societa per l'Incremento dei Rapporti Commerciali con l'Estero SpA. (SIRCE)
Via Larga 23
I-20122 Milan

JAPAN

C. Itoh & Co., Ltd.
Kitakyutaro-machi
Higashi-ku, Osaka

Marubeni Corp.
3, Moto-machi
Higashi-ku, Osaka

Mitsubishi Corp.
2, Marunouchi
Chiyoda-ku, Tokyo

Mitsui & Co., Ltd.
1, Nishi-shinbashi
Manato-ku, Tokyo

Nissho-Iway Co., Ltd.
3, Imbashi
Higashi-ku, Osaka

Sumitomo Shoji-Kaisha, Ltd.
5, Kitahama
Kighashi-ku, Osaka

NETHERLANDS

Handelsverkeer NV.
Westersingel 107
Rotterdam

Hollandsche Bank-Unie NV.
Herengracht 434-440
NL-1002 Amsterdam

Philipp Brothers (Holland) NV.
(see U.S. listing)
Prinses Irenestraat 39
NL-1011 Amsterdam

SPAIN

Focomin S.A.
Edificio Espana
Via Layetana 30
Barcelona

Fomento de Comercio Exterior SA.
Alfonso X, 5
Madrid

SWEDEN

The Axel Johnson Group
S-10375 Stockholm

Sukab AB.
Burger Jarlsgatan 2
S-10382 Stockholm

Transfer AB.
Sundyberg 1
S-17220 Stockholm

SWITZERLAND

Andre et Cie. SA.
Chemin Messidor 7
CH-1000 Lausanne

Contraco Holding und Finanz AG.
Chemin de Cap 3
CH-1006 Lausanne

Siber Hegner Holding Ltd.
Bellerivestrasse 17
CH-8034 Zurich

UNITED KINGDOM

Alcon (Compensation Trading) Ltd.
4 Audley Square
London W1Y 5DR

Biddle Sawyer & Co., Ltd.
(The Guinness Peat Group Ltd.)
32 St. Mary at Hill
London EC3 8DH

Bowater International Trading Co., Ltd.
(formerly Ralli Trading Finance Ltd.)
46 Berkeley Square
London W1X 5DB

Bremar Holdings Ltd.
Bremar House
27 Sale Place
London W2 1PT

Emerson Associated Ltd.
41/42 Berners Street
London WI P3AA

M. Golodetz (Overseas) Ltd.
Aldwych House
71/91 Aldwych
London WC2B 4HN

Inchcape & Co., Ltd.
40 St. Mary Axe
London EC3A 8EU

Kiril Mischeff Ltd.
Irwin House
118 Southwark Street
London SE1

Leopold Lazarus Ltd.
Gotch House
20-34 St. Bride Street
London EC4A 4DL

Tennant Trading Ltd.
9 Harp Lane
Great Tower Street
London EC3

UNITED STATES

Boles World Trade Corp.
1521 New Hampshire Ave., NW
Washington, DC 20036

Cicatrade U.S., Inc.
500 Park Avenue
New York, NY 10022

General Electric Trading Co.
570 Lexington Ave.
New York, NY 10022

M. Golodetz & Co., Inc.
666 Fifth Avenue
New York, NY 10019

ICC International
720 Fifth Avenue
New York, NY 10019

International Commodities Export Co.
(Division of ACLI International, Inc.)
717 Westchester Avenue
White Plains, NY 10604

Contitrade Services/Merban Americas Corp.
(wholly owned subsidiary of Continental Grain Co.)
One State Street Plaza
New York, NY 10004

Metallgesellschaft Services, Inc.
520 Madison Avenue
New York, NY 10022

Phillip Brothers, Inc.
1221 Avenue of the Americas
New York, NY 10020

Sears World Trade, Inc.
450 Fifth St., N.W.
Washington, DC 20001

United States Trading Co.
1605 New Hampshire Ave., NW
Washington, DC 20009

Woodward & Dickerson, Inc.
Woodward House
937 Haverford Road
Bryn Mawr, PA 19010

WEST GERMANY

BAFAG AG.
Sonnenstrasse 21
D-8000 Munich 2

Comex Aussenhandelgessellschaft mbH.
Immermannstrasse 40
D-4000 Dusseldorf

Industriehandel GmbH.
Hattersheimerstrasse 2-6
D-6000 Frankfurt/Main

Handelsverkehr GmbH.
(Part of the Siber Hegner Group, Switzerland)
Rossertstrasse 2
D-6000 Frankfurt/Main

Kieling & Co.
Martinistrasse 24
D-2800 Bremen 1

Marquard & Bahls & Co.
Kattrepelsbrucke 1
D-2000 Hamburg 1

appendix

F

Summary of Export Trading Company (ETC) Legislation*

*Prepared by the U.S. Department of Commerce's International Trade Administration, November 15, 1982.

On October 8, 1982, President Reagan signed into law the ETC legislation (Pub. L. No. 97-290, 96 Stat. 1233). Its purpose is to increase U.S. exports by establishing an office to promote the formation of ETCs, by permitting bankers' banks and bank holding companies to invest in ETCs, by reducing restrictions on export financing provided by financial institutions, and by modifying the application of the antitrust laws to certain export trade. It has four titles.

TITLE I—"ETC ACT OF 1982"

(To be codified at 15 USC §4001-4003.) Title I requires the Department of Commerce to establish an office to promote and encourage the formation of ETCs and to facilitate contact between producers of exportable goods and services and firms offering export trade services.

TITLE II—"BANK EXPORT SERVICES ACT"

(To be codified at 12 USC §§1841, 1843, 635a-4, and 372.)

ETC. An ETC is a company doing business in the United States principally to export goods or services produced in the United States or to facilitate such exports by unaffiliated persons. It can be owned by foreigners and can import, barter, and arrange sales between third countries, as well as export.

INVESTMENT. Recognizing that a successful ETC requires large infusions of capital, Title II permits equity investments (including 100 percent ownership) in ETCs by bank holding companies (BHCs),[1] Edge Act or Agreement Act corporations[2] that are subsidiaries of BHCs, and bankers' banks.[3] By structuring investment in this manner, Title II ensures adequate separation between a bank's involvement in export trade activities and its deposit-taking functions.

SAFEGUARDS. Title II also provides at least five safeguards to minimize potential risk to these ETC investors. First, it limits investment in an ETC to

---

[1]A BHC is a holding company which owns at least 25 percent of any bank subsidiary and which is registered with the Federal Reserve Board (FRB) under the BHC Act. BHC activities other than banking must be closely related to banking, such as credit cards or leasing.

[2]An Edge Act corporation is a corporation chartered, supervised, and examined by the FRB for the purpose of engaging in foreign or international banking or other foreign or international financial operations. It engages in certain limited deposit-taking functions in the United States. An Agreement Act corporation is a federally or state-chartered corporation that has entered into an agreement or undertaking with the FRB that it will not exercise any power that is impermissible for an Edge Act corporation.

5 percent of the banking entity's consolidated capital and surplus and restricts loans to an ETC to 10 percent of such capital and surplus. Second, it requires approval by the Federal Reserve Board (FRB) for the proposed investment in an ETC. If the FRB does not object within 60 days of written notice of the investment (90 days if extended), the investment can proceed. The FRB can only disapprove a proposed investment if there is (1) a need to prevent unsafe or unsound banking practices, undue concentration of resources, decreased or unfair competition, or conflicts of interest; (2) a finding that such investment would affect the financial or managerial resources of a BHC to an extent that is likely to have a materially adverse effect on the safety and soundness of any subsidiary bank of such BHC; or (3) a failure to provide certain required information. Third, a BHC or its subsidiaries investing in an ETC may not extend credit to the ETC or the ETC's customers on terms more favorable than those afforded similar borrowers in similar circumstances. Fourth, an ETC is restricted in its securities, agricultural production, and manufacturing activities. Its securities activities are limited to those of any BHC investing in it. Its agricultural modification and manufacturing activities are restricted to certain types of product modification necessary to comply with foreign requirements and to facilitate foreign sales. Fifth, if the ETC engages in certain types of speculation in commodities, securities, or foreign exchange, its BHC investor could be required by the FRB to divest the ETC or to comply with certain conditions.

EXPORT FINANCING. Recognizing that a successful ETC also needs access to external financing, Title II reduces restrictions on such export financing in two ways. First, it directs the U.S. Export–Import Bank to develop a new loan-guarantee program for loans to ETCs or other exporters extended by financial institutions or other creditors (public or private). These loans are to be secured by export accounts receivable or inventories or exportable goods. A major share of these loan guarantees should ultimately serve to promote exports from small, medium, and minority businesses or agriculture concerns. Second, Title II addresses the need for additional bank support of export trade by liberalizing restrictions on the amount of bankers' acceptances that a federally regulated bank may issue.[4]

TITLE III—EXPORT TRADE CERTIFICATES OF REVIEW

(To be codified at 15 USC §§4011-4021.)

---

[3]A bankers' bank is one whose only clients are other banks. Small banks form bankers' banks to offer a variety of services they could not independently offer. Inclusion of bankers' banks should encourage regional and small banks to invest in ETCs.

[4]Bankers' acceptances facilitate sales by substituting a bank's credit standing for that of the buyer, with the bank guaranteeing payment to the seller.

CERTIFICATION CRITERIA. In order to give exporters the greater certainty that may be necessary for joint export activities, while also protecting competitive principles, Title III establishes a review procedure and authorizes the issuance of a certificate which entitles the holder to a limited antitrust exemption. The certificate is issued by Commerce with Justice concurrence. Any "person" (not just an ETC) seeking to engage in export trade can apply for a certificate.[5] To qualify for a certificate, the applicant's export-related conduct must satisfy specified standards. It must not (1) substantially lessen competition or restrain trade in the United States or restrain the export trade of a U.S. competitor; (2) unreasonably enhance, stabilize, or depress prices in the United States; (3) be an unfair method of competition; or (4) reasonably be expected to result in the sale or resale in the United States of the exported goods or services.

PROTECTION CONFERRED BY CERTIFICATE. Once issued, the certificate, with appropriate terms and conditions, provides an exemption for the certified conduct from criminal and civil suits under both federal and state antitrust laws, with two exceptions: (1) persons injured by the certified conduct may sue for injunctive relief and actual damages for violation of the standards in Title III; (2) Justice may enjoin certified conduct threatening clear and irreparable harm to the national interest. However, Title III limits the first exception—private antitrust suits—in four ways. First, it permits a private litigant to recover only actual, not treble, damages. Second, the private litigant must file suit for a violation of the standards in Title III within 2 years of discovering the violation and not later than 4 years after the violation has occurred. Third, there is a presumption that the certified conduct complies with these standards. Fourth, an exporter with a certificate who successfully defends against the private suit will recover the cost of that suit plus a reasonable attorney's fee.

CERTIFICATION PROCESS. This certification program becomes operational 90 days after Commerce, with Justice concurrence, issues implementing regulations. Under the regulations, Commerce will be statutorily required to comply with the following time limits in processing an application:

1. Within 7 days of submission of the application, Commerce must forward to Justice a copy of the application, other information submitted with the application, and the other data, including the market share of the applicant.
2. Within 10 days of submission of the application, Commerce must publish a notice in the Federal Register identifying the applicant and describing the export-related conduct to be certified.

---

[5]A person includes an individual resident in the United States, a partnership or corporation (profit or nonprofit) created under the laws of the United States, a state or local government entity, or any association or combination, by contract or other arrangement, among such persons.

3. Within 90 days of submission of the application, Commerce must, with Justice concurrence, determine if the Title III standards are met and issue or deny a certificate of review. (The applicant can request expedited certification, but no certificate may be issued sooner than 30 days after notice is published in the Federal Register).
4. Within 30 days of receipt of the Commerce denial, the applicant can request reconsideration. Commerce, with the concurrence of Justice, must respond within 30 days of receipt of the request.

AMENDMENT, REVOCATION, JUDICIAL REVIEW. The regulations must also require the exporter to report to Commerce changes in matters specified in the certificate and must provide for amendment of the certificate. In addition, the regulations must provide for Commerce revocation or modification of the certificate where Commerce or Justice determines that the certified conduct no longer complies with the Title III standards. Finally, the regulations must permit a person aggrieved by the issuance, denial, amendment, or revocation of a certificate to sue in federal district court and to set aside those determinations within 30 days after they are made.

GUIDELINES. Commerce, with Justice concurrence, may publish guidelines that describe conduct with respect to which determinations have been or might be made, with a summary of the factual and legal bases underlying the determinations.

WEBB-POMERENE ASSOCIATIONS. Title III was enacted as separate legislation and does not affect the Webb-Pomerene Act, which provides a limited exemption from the U.S. antitrust laws for U.S. associations exporting goods. U.S. companies, therefore, can continue to register as Webb-Pomerene associations with the Federal Trade Commission (FTC). Unlike Title III, the Webb-Pomerene Act does not provide for export trade certificates of review, does not protect against the filing of private treble damage suits and does not cover the export of services or licensing.

TITLE IV—"FOREIGN TRADE ANTITRUST IMPROVEMENTS ACT"

(To be codified at 15 USC §6a and 45(a) (3). Title IV amends the Sherman Act and section 5 of the FTC Act to clarify that they do not apply to export trade unless there is a "direct, substantial, and reasonably foreseeable effect" on domestic or import commerce or on the export opportunities of a U.S. person. It does not amend the application of section 7 of the Clayton Act (including its incipiency standard) to joint ventures engaged in export trade.

Index